MW00772055

# STRANGE NEW ENGLAND

# STRANGE NEW ENGLAND

THOMAS D'AGOSTINO & ARLENE NICHOLSON

THE
History
PRESS

Published by The History Press
Charleston, SC
www.historypress.com

Copyright © 2021 by Thomas D'Agostino and Arlene Nicholson
All rights reserved

Photography by Arlene Nicholson except where noted.
Cover illustration by Jason McLean.

First published 2021

Manufactured in the United States

ISBN 9781467148979

Library of Congress Control Number: 2021934109

*Notice*: The information in this book is true and complete to the best of our knowledge. It is offered without guarantee on the part of the authors or The History Press. The authors and The History Press disclaim all liability in connection with the use of this book.

All rights reserved. No part of this book may be reproduced or transmitted in any form whatsoever without prior written permission from the publisher except in the case of brief quotations embodied in critical articles and reviews.

# Contents

# Contents

# Contents

# Acknowledgements

We would sincerely like to thank everyone who helped make this book possible. First and foremost, thank you to our dear friends Bob and Vickie Hughes for adventuring with us and taking photos of some of the places in the book; Magin and Greg Wood, who were always up for an adventure and creating illustrations for our books; authors Jim Ignasher, Joseph Citro, J.W. Ocker, Jeff Belanger and John William Tuohy; the Cavendish, Vermont Historical Society; Highlife Ski Club in Chittenden, Vermont; the Foster, Rhode Island Preservation Society; Emeritus Connecticut state archaeologist Nicholas Bellantoni; the *Berkshire Eagle*; the New England Historical Society; Terry McDermott, curator of the Wilmington, Massachusetts Town Museum; the Wilmington, Massachusetts Historical Society; Irene Morgan of the Franklin, Connecticut Historical Society; the Brattleboro, Vermont Historical Society; the Burrillville, Rhode Island Historical Society; the Cumberland Public Library; the Greenville Public Library; the *Observer Valley Breeze*; and many others who were instrumental in the making of this book who chose to remain anonymous.

# Introduction

Arlene and I have been asked on many occasions to compile stories of some of New England's most extraordinary and captivating people into one book; this is a compilation of their stories. Included in this book are some of the most incredible characters in the region's often bizarre history. In many cases, you will read about people who may seem to jump out of the most outre fiction, while in other cases, the local legend may have made them larger than life.

New England is a magical place where fact and fantasy seem to roam hand in hand. Legend and lore abound in this ancient region where stories of the devil, witches, vampires, ghosts and pirates are plentiful and ripe for the telling. Although some of the following accounts may be more common in New England's history, many others have slipped through the scribed leaves of time, becoming almost completely forgotten. This does not mean their accounts are less valuable or interesting. In some cases, you will not believe what you read while perusing through the following pages. On many occasions, we were astounded by the people who once lived and rambled the New England highways and byways. Yet, thorough research turned up records and accounts that proved beyond a shadow of a doubt that these people once lived and were a staple of the New England culture. From the veiled minister to the old Leather Man and even the evil and immortal Dr. Benton, these are the characters who were once the main topic of pubs and public gatherings around the region. These people and many more you will become familiar with as you enjoy this compilation of the strange and wonderful accounts etched into the fabric of what we call New England.

Some people in this book are part of an incident that became engraved into the area's history. To this day, their stories are told, perhaps in front of a crackling campfire with coyotes howling in the distance, setting the tone for the strange accounts rambling off the storyteller's tongue. Their lives may not have been remarkable, save for the one defining moment that made them part of the New England legend's landscape. This is why some of the accounts in this book are shorter than others, but the shorter tales are no less captivating than those that are more voluminous. Enjoy!

# Witches, Wizards and Vampires

## Tessa

The St. John River in northern Maine is the scene of this legend regarding witchcraft and the devil. The main character is a woman named Tessa.

Tessa's mother was believed to be a minion of the devil, having practiced witchcraft and spells. Her name was known far and wide, and the locals kept a wary eye on her, as they were sure the devil himself possessed her. When she died, the community's fearful folk decided to bury her in the local burying yard instead of unhallowed ground, for fear she may come back and curse them if they did otherwise. Several years later, the townspeople decided to relocate the cemetery. They exhumed the bodies for re-interment. Most had gone to bone and dust—all except Tessa's mother, who remained the same as she was when they first committed her to the earth. When they opened her coffin, the smell of lilacs permeated the air. Tessa was so amazed by this strange unearthly occurrence that she took a piece of her mother's flesh and placed it in a bottle on a shelf beneath a portrait of her deceased mother.

Tessa began to notice that on occasion, the portrait would be wet with tears, as if someone was weeping over it, and the bottle below would reek of lilac perfume. Neighbors soon became worried that Tessa was also a witch, as she used to disappear into the woods for long periods at a time. The deep woods of northern Maine were perfect for conjuring spells or meditating away from prying eyes. On one occasion, a neighbor walking by the river near her home found Tessa under the river's ice, smiling up toward the sky. This was when the townsfolk became convinced that she, like her mother, had become possessed by the dark one.

Meanwhile, in Tessa's home, windows flew open for no reason, and furniture would topple over. Any door with a crucifix above it would not open until the cross was removed. A black cat perched itself on her windowsill and could not be coerced away from its roost until a priest came and exorcised the known familiar of Satan. Tessa claimed that invisible demons began to claw at her. Witnesses who saw the marks left on her skin by these creatures believed it was the devil or one of his demons that caused the injuries.

Her father, who also witnessed these events, eventually died, and Tessa moved away to live with her uncle. The journey was not without several mishaps. The wagon wheels refused to stay fastened to the axles no matter how many times they stopped to repair them. At various times, the horses stopped and could not, under any condition, be coerced to plod forward. When she finally arrived at her new home, the house shook violently as if a great storm had taken to it.

It was only a few nights later that Tessa passed away of unknown circumstances. While the family prepared for her interment, her corpse mysteriously vanished from her room. Two years later, her body was found in a nearby old abandoned home, perfectly preserved. When the family came to claim it, they were overwhelmed by the smell of lilacs.

The funeral was once again arranged, and a local farmer brought a large ham to feed the attendees. No matter how many slices were served from the ham, it did not diminish in size. It seems the devil had one more prank up his sleeve. Astonished by this event, the farmer's wife took the wholesome ham home in a sack. When she opened the bag at home, all that remained was a large bone infested with maggots.

# MOLL PITCHER

*The day will come when the rockbound secrets of this cave will be revealed, and the world will be astounded by the priceless gems discovered.... The gold coins of all nations in boxes that, when opened, would contain ransom and riches enough to purchase an empire.*
*—from* The Celebrated Moll Pitcher's Prophecies *in regard to the lost treasure at Dungeon Rock*

New England is full of tales regarding witches, wizards and other seers who made their living through the telling of fortunes, but none is so recognized and once revered as Marblehead's own Moll Pitcher.

Moll Pitcher was the granddaughter of famed Marblehead wizard John Dimond (see later in the book), who was known to magically guide ships to safety during storms from atop Burial Hill in the small village. Moll was born Mary "Moll" Dimond (some spell it Diamond in more modern times) in 1738 in a house called the Old Brig at the foot of Burial Hill.

The stereotype of old hags crouching over crystal balls or cups of tea leaves certainly did not apply to Moll Pitcher. Unlike the images that have passed down from the generations of Moll being an old hag hunched over with a shawl covering her wretched frame, Moll was of medium stature, possessing an unusually large head, with a pale, thin face, arched eyebrows and long brown hair. She was a woman of intellect and could read people with the slightest movement of their body. If not a seer, she was genuinely gifted in reading personalities based on their actions and words.

Moll married a shoemaker by the name of Richard Pitcher on October 2, 1760, and had four children, John, Rebecca, Ruth and Lydia. They later moved to nearby Lynn, where she soon gained a reputation far and wide for telling fortunes. When her parents died in 1788, she inherited their property and continued to tell fortunes to all who sought her talents.

Birthplace of Moll Pitcher. *From the authors' collection.*

From royalty to rags, they came seeking the talents of Moll. Her cottage at the base of High Rock created the most appropriate atmosphere for her craft. She made predictions of events that would transpire up to ten, even twenty years after her tongue spewed the coming of such happenings. It was said that she even predicted the outcome of the Battle of Breed's Hill. Generals such as Burgoyne, Pitcairn, Gage and even Washington were among those who listened to the Oracle of Marblehead's predictions.

Sailors and sea captains came to see Moll before setting sail and would often postpone their journeys based on her predictions. In some cases, ships would sit at port empty for weeks until Moll gave a good prediction to sail. Nearly every port an American ship sailed into around the world knew of Moll Pitcher, and many would inquire of those who came from her jurisdiction of any news, good or bad. Businesspeople were wont to seek her advice before making important decisions.

Moll used tarot cards and read palms on occasion, but her primary fortunetelling method was derived from tea leaves. She would boil the leaves and dump them into the client's cup. From there, she would read the leaves that settled at the bottom of the cup. Their position revealed the fate of the inquirer. If the leaves fell scattered, the client would be unfortunate in love. If they fell crowded together, that meant happiness and wealth. If they arranged themselves in a series of lines, the client would live a long life and have many children. If but a few remained in the cup, the inquirer would die young.

Whether or not her predictions held much preciseness is a matter of modern conjecture, but those who sought her wisdom in her day took them as the wise words of a true seer. It is told that treasure hunters often sought out Moll for locations of lost booty. She would say something to the effect of, "Fools, if I knew where money was buried, do you think I would tell you where it is?"

Moll Pitcher died on April 9, 1813, and was buried in the West Lynn Burial Ground. Her stone states her name, Mary Pitcher, with her birth date of 1738. Her original grave was unmarked until 1887, when a proper monument was erected in her honor.

Molly may have gone to live with the spirits, but her predictions live on in a book published in 1895 called *The Celebrated Moll Pitcher's Prophecies*.

# The Magician of Marblehead

There are many varied tales of Edward (or John) Dimon (Dimond, Diamond). None of them always tend entirely to substantiate the other. One thing is a fact: Dimon existed and was known by many to be the "Magician of Marblehead" or "Wizard Dimon."

Dimon was born in 1641 and lived in Marblehead during the time of the Salem witch trials. He died in the same town in 1732 at age ninety-one. If one considers that he was known for his magical conjuring, then perhaps there were actual enchanters among the colonists during the witch hysteria, and maybe even before. Dimon, a retired sea captain, lived in a house near Burial Hill at 42 Orne Street called the Brig. It was in the graveyard where he would stand on the highest precipice during the raging storms and summon the powers that fueled his magic. Dimon, cape swirling in the howling winds and rains, harnessed the forces of nature while calling out to the ships at sea. Many sailors returning home swore they heard Dimon's voice reverberating over the wind and raging seas, guiding them toward safer waters. Some claimed to see his face in the storm clouds as his voice commanded their ship to calm waters.

According to legend, during these stormy encounters, he could see every vessel at sea that hailed from Marblehead, calling each ship and crew by name while commanding the wind and rain to subside until the ships were back in their home harbor. Many local families visited the wizard, hoping he could watch over their loved ones while they were away at sea. Some narrations regard him as a vengeful soul, stating that if he took favor on a certain captain, the ship would see port no matter how dreadful the storms it encountered; if the captain or crew had taken to his wrong side, the vessel was never seen again. This may be an embellishment of the tale because no one in the village could ever attest to him being anything but endearing to his fellow Marblehead mariners.

Dimon's powers were not all concentrated on the sea. A poor widow once came to Dimon for help regarding a thief who stole all her firewood. She was too impoverished to afford another load necessary to keep her meager cottage warm for the upcoming winter. Dimon used his powers to expose the culprit and then put a spell on the man to teach him a lesson. The thief was forced to walk back and forth from his house to the widow's house, from sunrise to sunset, with a massive log attached to his back that he could not remove. By morning, he was overly exhausted and had indeed learned a lesson on stealing from the poor, defenseless widow.

Burial Hill in Marblehead, where John Dimond performed his magic.

In no time, all the widow's wood, and then some, was returned with a sincere apology.

It is interesting to note that Dimon was the grandfather of the renowned fortuneteller Moll Pitcher (see above), born in Marblehead circa 1738 and died in Lynn in 1813. Pitcher came from a long line of seers and was known far and wide for her ability to read tea leaves and predict the future. She is buried in West Lynn Burial Ground, where a monument erected in 1887 marks her grave.

## GOODY COLE

The Salem witch trials of 1692 will go down in history as the most infamous witchcraft dilemma in America, but it was certainly not the first. Suspicions of witchery arrived with the *Mayflower* and gained impetus as the years of hard living caused the early superstitious settlers to blame witchcraft and Satan for their woes. In New Hampshire, there is one case of witchcraft that stands above the rest.

Eunice Cole came to America on February 20, 1637, with her husband, William. Little else is known, except that her husband was sixty-three years old at their arrival. There is no information on Eunice's date of birth. The couple was granted land in present Quincy, Massachusetts, but decided to follow Reverend John Wheelwright to New Hampshire in November 1637. He purchased land from the Indians and founded the town of Exeter. William Cole was one of the deed's original signers, but in 1640, the Coles decided to move to Hampton, where they settled for good.

Although they had forty acres of land in Hampton, they were still considered poor. Because of their social status, Mrs. Cole became known as Goodwife or "Goody" Cole, the proper term given to the lower-class married women of the period. Goody Cole was much outspoken for her time, and because of her free tongue, between 1645 and 1656, she appeared in court several times.

It was only a matter of time before Eunice Cole's vile and quick tongue would get her in trouble. A group of sailors found entertainment in poking fun at the old woman as she passed by their company. She shook her bony fist and cursed them before they set sail, saying they would never see home again. Upon their return, a storm whipped up and wrecked the ship as it passed the Isles of Shoals. Those who had overheard the venomous words of Eunice Cole felt convinced that she was responsible for the deed.

Goody Cole was arrested for witchcraft in 1657 and spent the next few years in a Boston prison. She was released in 1660 to care for her much older, ailing husband; this was short-lived because within a year, she was arrested and jailed on another charge of witchcraft.

William Cole died on May 26, 1662. Eunice was released shortly after but no longer owned land; the town had sold it to pay for her husband's care and her imprisonment. Angered by their actions, she let out a pyrotechnic display of expletives and curses on the townsfolk. Once again, she was arrested for using witchcraft to curse the town.

By 1671, Eunice was a poor, ailing old woman. The charitable townsfolk, realizing that her curses may have been nothing more than the words of an old hag, built a small cottage and reluctantly took turns caring for her. They did not fear being cursed as much as they feared paying for her imprisonment should she be arrested again. Either way, she lived the rest of her life in the small shack given to her; this is where the Tuck Museum and Founders Park sit today.

Although she was old and feeble, her tongue still lashed with the vigor of a young sailor. She found herself in front of the authorities a few more times, spending short terms in jail between 1671 and her death in 1680.

Although now pretty much convinced she was harmless, the townsfolk were not about to take any chances. When she died, the neighbors took her

Memorial founder's stone for Eunice Cole, Hampton's famous witch.

body outside and pushed it into a shallow grave. Before they put the dirt over her final resting spot, they drove a wooden stake through her heart in an attempt to finally exorcise the demons that resided within her in life. They also believed this would keep her in the grave. No one knows where she was buried, but it is assumed that her unmarked grave is in the Tuck Museum's close vicinity. The stake was not as effective as the citizens had hoped it would be, as her ghost has been seen roaming the area for many years.

The Tuck Museum placed an unmarked stone on the lawn as a memorial to Eunice Cole in 1963. When viewed from the park, it is quite uncanny how the stone resembles an older woman's crooked face wearing a hat or scarf about her head.

## TAMMY YOUNGER

The abandoned settlement of Dogtown Common in the heart of Cape Ann is famous for the illustrious and eccentric characters who resided within its boundaries. Almost every former Dogtowner has been praised in legend and lore. By all accounts, the tales of Tammy Younger are by far the most colorful.

Thomasine "Tammy" Younger was born on July 28, 1753, to William Younger and Lucy Foster. Tammy grew up in town, later living with her aunt Luce George in a house on Fox Hill at the entrance of Dogtown. As stated by Charles E. Mann in his book *The Story of Dogtown*, Tammy, "short and inclined to plumpness," had a small square window in the rear of the house with a wooden door. The sound of a wagon crossing the bridge over the brook was a signal for the door to fly open and Tammy to insist on a share of whatever was on the vehicle. Whether it was firewood, fish or produce, Tammy demanded her lot. If the poor traveler refused, Tammy and Aunt Lucy were known to bewitch the team hauling the load to the point where they froze in their tracks with their tongues hanging out until a fair portion was unloaded and brought into the house. Some claimed she could bewitch a pile of wood so it would not stay on a cart until an allotment was donated for the long winter ahead. She would often go down to the piers, threatening to put an evil eye on those who would not provide her with a bounty of fish.

Tammy smoked a pipe and partook in snuff. Many years after her home had fallen into ruin, an ornate snuff box was found in the cellar. It was most likely a gift from a sea captain or sailor who often visited Tammy to have their fortune told.

One day, a Dogtown youth passed along the back of Tammy's home. There, sitting in the autumn sun, was a pile of pumpkins freshly gained from another traveler. The youth picked one from the pile and sent the whole cache rolling into the brook. Tammy's window flew open, and "a torrent of vocal pyrotechnics" flowed from the woman's lips as the boy pulled every pumpkin from the water and piled them back where they previously sat.

Tammy Younger of Dogtown hexing an oxcart. *From the authors' collection.*

21

At one point, Tammy decided to part with two long teeth that protruded from her upper jaw. The teeth had become cumbersome to her, and she sought their removal. She summoned the local cobbler, Johnny Morgan Stanwood, to rid her of the fangs. She sat in a chair, and Stanwood began pulling one tooth until it gave way some. He drew it partly down and then commenced on the other one. When both were drawn down at equal length, he told her he could not pull them anymore. His practical joke was met with a barrage of language that left him stunned. He kept up his prank for a while longer before removing them completely.

Tammy died on February 4, 1829, at seventy-six years of age. The townsfolk, fearing she might come back and haunt them, had a fine coffin made with a pure silver nameplate on it. Cabinetmaker John Hodgkins was charged with the task of fashioning her coffin. Upon the casket's completion, a terrible storm rose with heavy rains and thunder pervading the hamlet. John was finishing a coat of beeswax on the coffin when his family entered the kitchen, refusing to go to bed while the coffin rested within the confines of the home. Even Mrs. Hodgkins, who was afraid of nothing, swore Tammy's spirit was already inside the box. John wrapped the coffin in a quilt and, in the pouring rain, carried it out to the barn.

The funeral was a major event, as the townspeople felt Tammy would have demanded. Instead of rum and cheap liquor, the best cordials and wines were served. It is not known if it was to please the spirit of Tammy or send her off with a bang. Guess there is no point in wondering now.

# Foster, Rhode Island: A Real Witch City

Everyone knows Salem, Massachusetts, as the "Witch City," but there is another place in New England that boasts several authentic witches among its past citizens. Foster, Rhode Island, is anything but a city. This sparsely populated small rural town in the northwestern section of the state is host to many legends, ghosts, witches and vampires and even houses the state's official haunt. Dolly Cole, the Brown family and Lonnie Davis are some of the most colorful characters in this wooded hamlet's history, as all have been labeled a witch at one point. Let's start with the legend of Dolly Cole.

A few legends surround Foster's Dolly Cole. One is that she was a witch who was burned with her home. Another is that she was a witch, and her child was thrown from the bridge into the nearby river. She jumped into the water to save the infant but vanished, never to be seen in a mortal frame again. Both the bridge and the river now bear her name. Another is that she was a vampire. One more legend claims that twenty-seven-year-old Dolly Cole was a murder victim, found in the woods near Tucker Hollow Road. There is a bit of fact in most of the stories.

Dorothy Cole of the hamlet of Hopkins Mills in Foster died in 1860 at ninety-one years, six months and four days of age. True, there is a bridge named after her, as well as a brook and a hill. That is because her family owned much of the area. Her house did burn down, but years after her death. Sadie Mathewson was murdered in 1899, not 1893, at the age of twenty-four. Perhaps that is the story that has been mixed with embellishment to create the Dolly Cole murder legend. The ghost of a woman, attributed to being Dolly Cole, has been seen standing near the bridge.

This author saw the ghost at about twelve years old while fishing with his father. It was the first full-blown apparition he had ever seen. It was of a woman in a white gown with bare feet leaning into the pool, drawing water into a wooden bucket. She then floated away down the path. He would later find out that the ghost of Hopkins Mills is Betsey Grayson, who died on December 20, 1860, while attempting to fetch water from the rushing river with her wooden bucket. The current pulled her in, and she hit her head on the rocks in the river and subsequently drowned.

Some have seen a woman near Tucker Hollow Road's gun club and say that spirit is Dolly Cole. But that is also where Aunt Lonnie (Lannie) Davis once resided. The townsfolk feared her as a witch and steered clear of her when she was out and about. (See chapter "Curses.")

Dolly Cole may or may not have been a witch, but Foster did have its share of them. For instance, Isiah Brown married Peggy Hurley (or Herlihy) of Ireland. She was well known for her spells, charms and herbal remedies. Isiah died in 1897 and is buried at Foster Cemetery #034. Peggy may also be buried there, but it is not on record; however, there are a few stones with no inscriptions. Old-timers told tales of another set of witches who would scare anyone they did not hold in good favor by cursing them or making items fly off walls and shelves in their homes. They were also known to make rocking chairs sway frantically or cause pictures on walls to shake violently. Abby and Whaley Brown were called the witches of Jerimoth Hill. The two sisters were feared far and wide for their ability to cast spells and cause items to fly about rooms. The sisters are buried at Foster Cemetery #001 on the Rhode Island–Connecticut border. Abby was born in 1803 and died in 1875. On a few occasions, visits to the cemetery did not turn up a Whaley Brown among the stones, nor any record of that name during research. A Phila was born

The witches of Jerimoth Hill, Foster, Rhode Island. *Courtesy of Observer Publications.*

in 1805 and died in 1880, and a Pardon Brown was born in 1792 and died in 1869; they would have been about the same age as Abby. Perhaps Whaley was a nickname. Whatever the case, the two sisters were known as witches almost into the twentieth century.

## EXETER, RHODE ISLAND: THE "LAST" VAMPIRE

*EXHUMED THE BODIES—TESTING A HORRIBLE*
*SUPERSTITION IN THE TOWN OF EXETER—BODIES OF*
*DEAD RELATIVES TAKEN FROM THEIR GRAVE*
*They had all died of Consumption, and the belief was that live flesh and blood would be found that fed upon the bodies of the living.*

This was just one of the headlines that graced the front of newspapers around the country in March 1892. The story recounted the gruesome account of the Brown family of Exeter, Rhode Island, and their deadly "brush" with vampirism. One of the eeriest chapters in New England's history concerns the vampire plague that struck the region. It dates back to 1784, when a Willington, Connecticut resident named Isaac Johnson disinterred his two children and performed a sort of exorcism, as per the request of a foreign doctor whom the news labeled a "quack." The children's bodies were exhumed and their vitals removed and burned. They then searched for a vine that grew from one coffin to another. The belief was that if such a vine existed and was cut from the coffins, then the spread of death would cease.

For the next 108 years, scores of families exhumed their loved ones, hoping that superstition and folklore would work where medicine had failed. The fear of "spectral ghouls," as they were called, feeding on their family members was a real terror in New England. Consumption, the current name for tuberculosis, was the actual culprit, yet it managed to make its way into the New England folks' superstitious minds in the form of a vampire.

The last known case of the New England vampire occurred in 1892 in the little hamlet of Exeter. This rural village was no stranger to the vampire's grasp, having recorded a similar case in 1799. Apple farmer Stutley Tillinghast had a foreboding dream of losing half of his orchard. His daughter Sarah soon became ill with consumption and died. Within six months, four more of his fourteen children died of the dreaded disease, each one claiming that Sarah came to them in the night, sucking their life away. Five fieldstone graves in the family plot are a grim reminder of how this family died in such rapid succession; Stutley had no time to procure proper stones. When another child became ill, family and friends gathered to face their dilemma. It was decided that a vampire was at work, and on a misty morning, a small group assembled at the cemetery and exhumed the bodies of the children. Most of them had already begun going back to the earth, but Sarah, the first to succumb to consumption, had not shown one sign of decay. This was more than enough to convince the crowd they had found their vampire. They cut out her vitals and burned them, then re-interred the deceased. The sixth child died anyway. It was concluded that she was too far gone to save. In the end, Stutley's dream of losing half his orchard had been a foretelling of losing half his children. The Tillinghast account is fascinating indeed, but it was the case of Mercy Brown that would bring the New England vampire into world attraction.

Mercy's mother, Mary Eliza, died on December 8, 1883, at the age of thirty-six, followed by Mercy's sister Mary Olive on June 6, 1884, at age twenty. When her brother Edwin became ill, he left for the curing waters of Colorado Springs. During his absence, Mercy contracted the dreaded consumption. Her illness lasted only three months before it took her to the grave on January 17, 1892. Her remains were placed in the keep at the Chestnut Hill Baptist Cemetery, as the ground was frozen until the spring thaw allowed for a proper burial. Edwin returned feeling a little better, but soon his condition worsened. The townsfolk suspected that one of the deceased family members was feeding on his lifeblood in the form of a vampire.

George Brown scoffed at the idea that one of his own might be a vampire, yet perpetual insistence by his neighbors and Edwin growing paler by the day made him consider the only cure left: an exorcism of the suspected culprit. He agreed to exhume his family under the direction of a medical doctor present. On March 17, 1892, some of the locals met at the cemetery to find their vampire. Dr. Harold Metcalf of Wakefield, Rhode Island, presided over the exhumations. George Brown was not present, as he believed there was no vampire to be found. They disinterred the remains of Mary Eliza and Mary Olive, but the earth had long reclaimed their flesh, leaving only bones. They then opened the keep and removed the coffin containing Mercy. When they abstracted the lid, they all stepped back, gasping in fright. Not only had she stirred while in the coffin, but it appeared her hair and nails had grown. She was still pale as the day she died and showed signs of dried blood around her lips.

The keep at Chestnut Hill Cemetery where Mercy Brown was placed until spring burial.

Mercy Brown, the "last" New England vampire.

When they cut her heart open, it is reported that fresh blood trickled out; this, to the local swain, was a sure sign she had recently fed. Her heart and lungs were then removed and burned on a nearby rock. The ashes were fed to Edwin with some medicine in the hopes that it would eradicate the disease that was slowly consuming him.

The cure failed, and Edwin passed away on May 2, 1892. News of the gruesome event spread like wildfire across the country and even into Europe; this was the last known exorcism for vampires in New England. Knowledge of the disease soon came to the rural towns and marked an end to the grotesque ritual of exhuming the dead and burning their vitals to rid families of the curse that took them to their graves.

An interesting footnote about this case is that newspaper clippings about the Mercy Brown incident were found among his possessions when Bram Stoker died. In 1897, he wrote *Dracula* using the accounts of Mercy Brown along with other people and places. One thing to note is that the main town in his book is called Exeter.

# JB 55

Many scholars and historians know New England as the vampire capital of the world. From 1784 to 1892, many cases of vampires and subsequent exorcisms to eradicate them were well documented in town ledgers, newspapers, private journals and history books. The exact number of vampire cases may never be known, but the scare was real and widespread throughout the region.

We now know the cause of the vampire scare was consumption, or tuberculosis, as we now call it. The dreaded disease was highly contagious, sometimes wiping out whole families within a year or two. There was no treatment, and doctors had no answers. That is when the dire New England folk turned to superstition and folklore for a cure.

Scores of deceased family members were exhumed and checked for signs that their spirits, known as "spectral ghouls," rose from the grave each night to feed on a family member before returning to the tomb to nourish the rotting corpse that lay in repose. The only cure thought to be effective was to cut out the suspected ghoul's heart, liver and lungs and burn them. For good measure, the afflicted would then be compelled to mix the ashes with medicine and drink the concoction in hopes of ridding the evil that had fallen upon them.

In modern times, the written word was all we had to substantiate this scare, but then something happened. In 1990, three children playing in the sandbanks of a gravel facility in Griswold, Connecticut, accidentally unearthed some remains of coffins and bones. A few skulls tumbled down the hillside, sending the frightened trio running and screaming.

Upon investigation, it was discovered that the remains were part of a long-abandoned cemetery. Investigators were called in, and plans to move the remaining burials commenced. The cemetery was found to be a burial lot with five men, eight women, fourteen children and one empty grave. The graves were numbered and sketched for reburial. The operation went well until they reached grave no. 4.

When opened, it was found to be lined with stone slabs as if to keep something out or in. When the top slab was removed, the initials "JB 55" were found nailed with tacks into the coffin's top. When the coffin lid was removed, the crew found the skeleton was rearranged in a strange skull and crossbones pattern. The thighbones had been removed and placed over the rib cage. Some ribs had also been removed, as if a primitive autopsy had taken place. The skull was decapitated from the rest of the skeleton and placed on the rib cage. The discovery dumbfounded archaeologists and researchers on the scene until further research concluded that the man had died of tuberculosis.

The reason for the strange exorcism was the belief that he may have been one of the suspected undead. When the family attempted to rid themselves of the vampire, JB had decomposed to the point where only his skeleton remained, which led the fearful folk to use a different approach to exorcising their bloodsucking ghoul.

*Left*: Part of the coffin lid from the grave of JB 55. *Courtesy of Nicholas Bellantoni.*

*Below*: Walton Cemetery relocation in an undisclosed location.

Studies of the bones showed lesions from the disease and other injuries the person sustained during his lifetime. The "55" may have been his age when he died. But who was JB 55? Thanks to modern science, the country's best-known example of this eighteenth- and nineteenth-century panic now has a name. Thirty years have passed since the only tangible example of vampirism in New England was discovered. As a result of intense research and modern DNA testing, the full name of this poor individual who suffered at the hands of a most horrible disease, was exhumed and defiled is now known. His name, according to experts, was John Barber.

These modern methods are more than a milestone, as we not only have physical evidence of the vampire scare that plagued New England centuries ago, but we have a name to match. Two other coffins found initialed with the same tacks were next to Barber's. One had "NB 13" nailed into it. Local historical research uncovered a local newspaper notice from 1826 reporting the death of a twelve-year-old boy named Nathan Barber, whose father was John Barber. Nathan had died just before his thirteenth birthday. Perhaps the ritual took place to save him or the other person in the coffin labeled "IB 45." Either way, our most famous physical case of vampires in New England now has a name, and all that is left is to find the exact date he died and why he was exorcised.

# Mary Nasson

Many people visit Old York, Maine, for its historical content. Several buildings boast legends and stories typical of early New England. Alongside one of the buildings is a small burying yard with many famous local names. Several yards from the cluster of stones, sitting alone and ominous, there lies a single grave; this may not seem so strange at first, but the presence of a great lintel laid across the grave makes one wonder why the stone lies on top. Even more, why is the grave site so far removed from the rest of the burials?

Mary Nasson was a noted and respected herbalist in the community. Because of her knowledge in healing with plants, she became known as the "White Witch of York." Mary was born in 1745 and grew up in York Village. She married Samuel Nasson and settled down to a life of farming and assisting others in the little hamlet. Mary was also known to be a skilled exorcist who rid many houses of demons and demonic possessions during

The slab-covered grave of Mary Nasson, York's "White Witch."

her time on earth. Her time was relatively short, though, because Mary died on August 18, 1774, at the age of twenty-nine.

Her grave sits alone in a far corner of the cemetery. A likeness of her is carved into the stone. It is also the only one in the burial yard with a giant granite slab over the top. If the legend is correct, York's people placed it there to keep the White Witch from rising out of her tomb. A more logical reason may have been to keep the livestock from accidentally digging her up. Farmers, on the condition their livestock could still graze among the stones, often donated land for these early burial grounds to the villages. The townsfolk were in charge of the upkeep of their family grave sites. After Mary died, her husband moved several miles away to Sanford, making it very difficult to tend to her grave regularly. If the stone was placed there to keep the livestock away, it served its purpose. If it was laid there to keep the York witch from rising, it did not work as well as the townsfolk hoped, at least not in the present era.

Her ghost is reported to roam the area where she is buried. Legends persist of her stone being cool to the touch, yet the granite slab is warm, almost hot to the hand when laid on it. Some have sworn that the crows that frequent the graveyard seek out her grave in particular, as they are her familiars.

Her ghost is often seen wandering the burial ground and the small playground across the street. Mary had two children: Peter, born in 1766, died in 1784 at the age of twelve; and Susannah, born in 1768, died in 1793 at the age of twenty-five.

Children have spoken of the nice young lady who pushes their swings in the playground. Mothers have even seen the swings moving while the children laugh and converse with an unseen entity. When asked, they always say Mary is pushing the swings and playing games. If it is Mary, perhaps she has stayed behind to play with the children she never got to see grow up in her lifetime.

# CUMBERLAND'S STRANGE REQUEST

Town council meetings can have some pretty strange requests. Sometimes it is a noise ordinance to stop peacocks from screeching. It may be a citizen who does not like certain signs posted or cars parking on the street. One of the strangest requests comes early in our nation's history. The request was at the very first town council meeting held in Cumberland, Rhode Island, on February 8, 1796. This is how it is written:

> *Mr. Stephen Staples of Cumberland appeared before this council and prayed that he might have liberty granted unto him to dig up the body of his dofter* [daughter] *Abigail Staples late of Cumberland single woman deceased in order to try an experiment on Lavina Chace wife of Stephen Chace which said Lavina was sister to said Abigail deceased which being duly considered it is voted And resolved that the said Stephen Staples have liberty to dig up the body of the said Abigail deceased and after trying the experiment as aforesaid that he bury the body of the said Abigail in a deasent* [decent] *manner.*

That is what was entered into town records. We know that Abigail Staples was born on January 26, 1773, and died about 1795, most likely of consumption. Lavina was born on June 26, 1762. She was married at the time of the request.

Whole families were wiped out by the malady that held New England in the grip of fear for over a century. The people feared loved ones who had died from the disease were returning in spirit and feeding upon the family's surviving members. As long as the body remained whole or decomposing in the grave, the spirit would feed upon the living and return to the grave

The much-neglected Staples lot in Cumberland where Abigail may have been buried.

to nourish the body. Stephen Staples happened to be one of those who believed his daughter Abigail may have been returning from the grave to claim her sibling.

Incidentally, there is no record regarding the exact nature of Mr. Staples's experiment or the outcome. The Staples lot in Cumberland has many fieldstone markers, so the precise whereabouts of Abigail's grave is also lost to antiquity.

Next time you attend a town council meeting, think about citizens' strange requests and think back to the request once asked in Cumberland. I am sure they will not compare.

## DOGTOWN'S EASTER CARTER

Dogtown, originally known as the Commons Settlement, tenanted various colorful characters during its life as a town. One such character was a woman named Esther "Easter" Carter.

Easter lived at what is now known as 15 Dogtown Road. A carved boulder marks the former location of her home. Easter had the only two-story house in the Commons Settlement. The clapboard home held together by wooden pegs was, by Dogtown standards, quite a luxurious abode. Despite this appellation, Easter was very poor but nevertheless a generous old soul. Charles Mann states that she was "quite respectable and undeserving of the distinction which classes her with other Dogtown dames of doubtful reputation."

The young of nearby Annasquam and Riverdale would trek up to her home for picnics and her famous boiled cabbage. While others tolerated the wild berries and meager sustenance the settlement naturally afforded them, Easter would have no part of it. "I eats no trash," was her retort for such scanty meals.

Like so many other Dogtowners, Easter was a fortuneteller and would often tell the young folks fortunes, no doubt in such a way that would make the walk home for a young lad and lass more romantic in the moonlit Cape Ann. Easter Carter was also somewhat of the village nurse, caring for the locals when they were sick. Her knowledge of herbs and spices for the healing of ailments made many a Dogtowner, as Becky Rich would say, "springish" once more.

Since most Dogtown folks did not need a two-story home, the second story of Easter's house was occupied by a mulatto woman named "Old

Easter Carter's Dogtown cellar hole.

Ruth." Old Ruth was a character in her own right. Being poor like the rest of the village, she found work as a laborer and dressed in men's clothing. She went under the moniker of "Tie" as well as "John Woodman." Building stone walls and completing heavy farm labor became her chief means of employment. She was frequent in saying that she had always worked outdoors and wore men's clothing as a result of her chosen occupation. It was not until she was taken to the poorhouse to live out her last days that she was grateful to oblige society's customs and wear skirts. A ledge behind Easter Carter's former home is called Ruth's Ledge in her honor.

One time, a group of young people came to visit Easter, bringing a collage of wallpaper to decorate her home. They put up the wallpaper, and Easter was pleased with the effect, even though the paper was of many various designs. Easter died around 1833. Like many of her fellow villagers, she had been taken from Dogtown's derelict homes to the poorhouse. If you decide to visit Dogtown, you will find the small boulder with the number 15 carved in it on Dogtown Road, not far from the entrance past the gate. You may even hear the voice of a Dogtown "witch" whispering in the wind.

# MOLLY BRIDGET

In the years surrounding the American Revolution, a woman named Molly Bridget was known far and wide for her powers as a witch. Molly made her name by telling fortunes and casting spells, often notorious ones for her time. Many were aware of her nefarious reputation and desired that she stay away from their municipality. While in Boston, she was approached by the authorities with a warning to leave the city at once. "Why, sir?" asked Molly.

"Is not your name Molly Bridget?" asked one officer.

Her quick reply was, "No, sir. Do you think I am such a despicable creature as Molly?"

Molly did leave Boston, arriving in 1782 in Portsmouth, New Hampshire, where she was given shelter at the local almshouse. Soon after, the residents, especially superintendent Clement March, noticed that the pigs on the premises started acting strangely, almost as if they had been bewitched.

March became convinced Molly had put a spell on them as they ravaged the gardens and continually wandered out of their sty, for it was known that no fence could contain that which is possessed by a witch. March considered burning her at the stake but feared being arrested for murder. He also feared that the pigs were just the beginning of what Molly was capable of while at the almshouse.

Many other alternative rituals could be used to rid the place where a witch resided, but none was available. Upon researching his options, March came across a remedy where a witch's spell could be broken by burning the object of the possession. March was not about to burn the pigs but came up with a hopeful solution. He cut off the very tips of their tails and ears in an attempt to purge the bewitchery from them.

March gathered up some leaves and brush and lit a fire. As soon as the pigs' tails and ear tips were tossed into the blaze, Molly began bouncing from room to room in a wild frenzy. She then rushed to her room. As the flames drew cold, so did Molly's life. By the time the fire was out, Molly laid dead on her bed.

On the day of her funeral, a terrible storm arose, which is common when witches are buried. March was grateful he could save his pigs and rid the town of one of the more notorious witches in the region.

# Curses

## Aunt Lonnie Davis

Foster, Rhode Island, seems to command a great deal of attention when it comes to ghosts, witches and vampires. Old maps of the town contain strange location monikers named after the peculiar folk who graced those locales. Names such as Witch Hill, Witch Rock and Ghost Lot are but a few of the area's sobriquets named after its resident legends. One of Foster's more prominent was a woman named Mary "Aunt Lonnie" (some say Lannie) Davis.

Aunt Lonnie lived on Tucker Hollow Road on the Scituate/Foster border. She was a recluse thought by many to be in league with the evil one. Lonnie would push her cart down Route 6 to the village of Hopkins Mills, where she would procure her necessities before pushing the full cart back up the steep hill toward home. Occasionally, an unwary youth would offer assistance, only to be spurned with an evil eye. Lonnie seemed to have an aversion with the townsfolk to the point where she not only avoided contact with them but demanded that upon her death, her home be demolished and her property forever remain unimproved. It was a strange request with an even stranger consequence. She swore if so much as two boards remained nailed together, she would haunt the area until her wish was granted in full.

When Aunt Lonnie died, the townspeople failed to adhere to her demands and soon paid the price for their action. Whenever someone passed by the abandoned property, unearthly screams would emanate from the home, and a cold breath would send a chill down their backs. If anyone dared venture onto the cursed land, a voice would whisper in their ear accompanied by a bone-chilling wind. If this was not enough to convince the trespasser to vacate her property, a vigorous push by unseen hands sent the intruder fleeing in fear.

It came to pass that the only way the neighbors could be rid of Aunt Lonnie was to fulfill her last wish. The home was torn down, and no two boards remained nailed together. They finally were rid of the curse—or so they thought. The

Mary "Aunt Lonnie" Davis's neglected gravestone.

land where Lonnie Davis once lived is now called the "Ghost Lot" and continues to be haunted centuries later. A 1947 map exhibits the location of the plot that is aptly named. There is a foundation where Aunt Lonnie's home once stood, and that parcel of land remains untouched.

Mary Davis and her husband, Joseph, are buried in the Tucker Hollow Cemetery very close to the Ghost Lot. Perhaps Aunt Lonnie was a nickname given to Mary; Lonnie could have been her middle name. Her birth date is unknown, but her death date, 1799, is clearly marked on the crude stone marker that sits among the brush and growth in the old burying yard.

# THE HAYDEN FAMILY CURSE

Do you believe in curses? Many scoff at such rants brought forth from the tongues of those who feel wronged for one reason or another. In the case of the Hayden family of Albany, Vermont, most had no chance to render their opinion until it was too late.

In 1798, William Hayden married Silence Dale. They moved from their Braintree, Massachusetts residence to the region of Craftsbury, Vermont, thanks to the financial aid of Silence's wealthy mother, Mercie Dale. Mercie was, at the time, a widow and thought it wise to move in with the young couple. William had grand plans for their future and began borrowing money from the aging old woman with the promise of paying back every penny. This scenario became a regular incident in which Mercie complied for some time, yet had not received a single shilling of recompense.

With money borrowed from Mercie, William purchased a large tract of land that would later become the town of Albany. With this, William began to work on business ventures, build a mansion and live the life of a noble, all on his mother-in-law's savings. Every time Mercie demanded her money from William, he would come up with some excuse to defer the payment.

The day came when she refused any more advances on his loans and demanded what was owed to her. After all, he had a grand mansion, lots of land and several other holdings. This was when things began to go wrong for Mercie. She suddenly took ill. As her condition worsened, she feared her son-in-law was poisoning her, but her daughter refused to believe William could be so nefarious. Desperate and ailing, Mercie arranged to room with her friend Sally Rogers who lived nearby. She knew her son-in-law was trying to be rid of her so he would not have to pony up the vast amount of money he owed her. As she left the splendid mansion she had so unwillingly funded, she placed a curse on William, stating, "The Hayden family shall perish in the third generation, and the last to die shall do so in great poverty."

William laughed off the curse made by the old woman as the ranting of a delirious hag. Mercie died a short time later and was buried in the Rogers family lot. Perhaps she intended the curse to take effect long after her daughter was gone to relieve her of such grief in her lifetime. Soon after Mercie's passing, William's luck began to change. Some of his more dubious dealings started to catch up with him, and he found himself fleeing Albany, eventually settling in Farnsworth, New York, where he died in 1846, an impoverished, broken man. Out of the nine children he had fathered, only two, one son and one daughter, reached adulthood.

His daughter Arathuza died childless at the age of sixty-four. His son William Jr. grew to manhood and married. His mother, Silence Dale Hayden, still living in Albany, died in 1872 at ninety-four. This was the end of the first generations of the Hayden family curse. William Jr. married and started a family of his own but was bewildered as his wife, Azubah, gave birth to all daughters. Finally, the fifth child, William Henry, was born, and he was sure that the now decades-old curse was nothing more than a bunch of bunk perpetuated by unfortunate coincidence.

William Henry (known as Henry) became successful in business, building a great house with a suspended ballroom on the top floor to entertain the socialites of the day. Will and Azubah's five children—Henry, Julia, Mary, Azubah and Alvina—marked the third generation of William Sr. Hayden's family, the target of Mercie's curse. That was when the curse took its final hold on the Haydens. All of Will and Azubah's children either died young or failed to produce male heirs. The only son, Henry, began to exhibit signs of insanity yet managed to marry, having three girls and one son. All of them died without producing another generation of Haydens, his son dying in 1871 at the tender age of five.

William Jr. grew old and feeble, watching the family fortune erode under the unstable Henry's control, the last male heir of the family name. Henry died in 1910 of a cerebral hemorrhage. The last person of the family lineage alive was his daughter Armenia Mamie Hayden. On February 20, 1927, she died poverty-stricken, unmarried and alone, thus ending the Hayden name and fulfilling the family curse. The old mansion still exists and is now a private residence. There are stories and accounts for the possibility of it being haunted, but they may just be stories to accompany the impetus of the curse. Subsequent owners have attested that there is nothing paranormal within the mansion, which may strengthen the curse's power that wiped out the Hayden family forever, including their ghosts.

# THE CURSE OF MICAH ROOD'S APPLES

This little tale of New England's myths and mysteries is a perennial favorite of the region. It is also true. Sit back and raise the flame on your lantern so you can see the shadows dancing on the walls as you read about Franklin, Connecticut's cursed apples.

Many do not believe in curses, as such vexes were tales designed to keep children in their beds long after the lights were drawn. In Franklin, many of the old-timers not only believe in curses, but some of them have actually ingested the remnants of a particular act of vengeance wrought upon a man over three centuries ago. There is a place where an apple tree once bore fruit with what appeared to be a single drop of blood in the center. Do not look for the tree now; it is long gone, but the legend and accounts that follow will live as an eternal reminder of the price of greed and murder.

Micah Rood, born in 1653, was a farmer in what was once called Nine Mile Square or Norwich-West-Farms, presently Franklin, Connecticut. Rood married Sarah Dayns (born on January 9, 1655) on January 15, 1693, and had three children, Mary, Micah and Joseph. His farm rambled along the Peck Hollow section of the settlement. The youngest son of Thomas Rood, Micah, came to settle there in 1699. By some accounts,

Rood was known to be friendly and outgoing, always taking time to help anyone in need. Others say he was a mean and nasty brute. One thing was sure: Rood's apple orchard was the finest and best tended in the region.

One December evening, a peddler named Horgan passed along the edge of Rood's farm. Many of the local housewives and working gentry eagerly awaited his semiannual visits to see what wares he had in his bag for sale to the good people of the town. In the seventeenth, eighteenth and even nineteenth centuries, peddlers were the common shopping medium. These roving stores wandered the countryside selling everything from pots and pans to trinkets and jewelry. Horgan seemed to have a fine array of items that would make almost any man want to rifle his sack. By all known accounts, the itinerant peddler sold much of his wares that day and now possessed a hefty pouch of money collected from his dealings. The next versions are indeed a matter of conjecture as to what transpired next. Some say that the peddler, on a roll, decided to try his luck at Rood's home, while others claim he was coerced into the house by Rood for reasons no good. Either way, the peddler was found the next day under one of Rood's apple trees with his head split open, his sack empty and his money pouch gone.

All fingers pointed toward Rood, but he vehemently denied any wrongdoing. In fact, he brought to the attention of the authorities that Horgan had spoken of two men who attempted to waylay the traveling salesman at the Blue Horse Tavern the day prior. Rood even let the authorities search his home, yet they found no sign of any violence or the peddler's property. Horgan was buried in the Potter's Field. Although the villagers were convinced Rood had something to do with his demise, they had no evidence, and the matter was soon put aside.

Spring wore on, and Rood's orchard once again began to prosper. No one could prove that Rood may have killed the peddler, but nature was about to throw a strange light on the suspicion of the townsfolk. When the flowers bloomed, the apple trees blossomed with their usual sweet-smelling white flowers, except for one tree. The tree where the peddler was found bore red flowers. Though odd, no one gave it much thought until August brought the fruits of labor forth. The townsfolk were quite astonished when they found the apples that came from that particular tree in Rood's orchard had a curious nature to them. When broken open, there was a red globule in the center that resembled a drop of blood. Every apple on the tree had within, the bloodstain of the man who was murdered so hideously. The people began to call them "Mikes," for although they concealed the strange crimson blot within, they were unusually delicious.

As for Rood, he began a slow and cryptic deterioration of both physical and mental health. The once vivacious soul was now a frail recluse. Always fearful and melancholy, he refused to eat and began wasting away. Neighbors reported hearing his screams in the night, and when they crept to his window, he was seen pacing to and fro in the darkest hours in front of a solitary candle. Within a short time, his farm withered along with his will to live. Every tree soon gave up the ghost but one. Year after year, that cursed tree bore the silent damnation of the apples with the bloody heart. Many came to believe that the peddler's spirit had come to roost on the branches of the tree, thus tainting the fruit it bore. One season, a daring youth stole into Rood's orchard and began to loot the infamous tree of its harvest. Rood offered him all of the tree's fruit, screeching, "Take the whole lot, boy, I don't want the accursed things!"

Rood's condition worsened, his fences fell into ruin, his home became a neglected relic and his barn decayed and swayed with the valley breezes that swept through the countryside. It is said he was terrified to work in the fields, for the wraith of the peddler was always waiting there to torture him for his deed.

In 1717, he was given the task of maintaining the meetinghouse, and in return, the congregation compensated him with a peck of corn from each family. Having long given up on living, his torturous existence continued, yet there bore no confession from his lips as to what happened to Peddler Horgan so many years ago. The bloody apples still poured from the tree that sat on the once fertile land now overgrown with brush and bramble.

In 1727, it came to pass that Rood needed constant attention, as he had become too feeble to care for himself. A historic record entered into the church society states as follows: "July 5, 1727. The inhabitants do now, by their vote, agree to allow each man that watches with Micah Rood, two shillings per night. Also to those who have attended to sd Rood by day, three shillings per day."

Micah Rood finally passed away in December 1728. It is written that he died in a chair overlooking the tree that bore the bloody fruit of vengeance. On December 17, 1728, the society paid four shillings to Jacob Hyde for digging Rood's grave. As for his wife, she died on May 10, 1749, at the age of ninety-four. His three children seem to have faded into history.

However, the tree lasted as a living monument to the unsolved crime for two more centuries, still bearing forth its peculiar harvest until the hurricane of 1938 finally blew the relic down. Several attempts were made to cultivate the "Mikes" by grafting the branches and roots with other strains. Still,

Old colonial map of Norwich, West Farms, 1663–1725. The arrow points out Rood's farm. *Photo by Arlene Nicholson from authors' collection.*

there is no record of whether anyone ever successfully reproduced the apples that silently and eternally condemned Micah Rood for his evil deed. Some say a few trees were grafted successfully and bear traces of the bloody apple. Take a ride into Franklin and visit some of the orchards around harvest time. Maybe, just maybe, you will find an apple with a blood-red heart. If so, then it is clear that the curse of Micah Rood is still alive in those delicious apples that gave so many taste buds pleasure and one man eternal pain.

# Rachel's Curse

In Plymouth, Massachusetts, there once lived an old woman the locals called Aunt Rachel. She earned a modest living telling fortunes to the locals, but it was mostly sailors who called upon her talents of predicting the weather and their future.

One day, a few sailors called upon her for her talents, and she immediately recognized one as a fellow villager. The others she knew to be of shady character, and Rachel chided the local for keeping society with the "rogues" he was with. One of the other men interrupted her lecture by stating, "None of your slack old woman or I will put a stopper on your gab."

It was then Rachel began calling them mooncussers—those who lure ships with false beacons onto rocks or shore for plunder. She looked the man straight in the eye and cursed, "He who rides the pale horse be your guide, and you be of the number who follow him."

That night, Rachel's house mysteriously burned to the ground, almost taking her with it. A few days later, the brig with the men who had visited her previously was ready to set sail, and Rachel joined the townsfolk to see it off. The owner of the brig offered his deepest sympathies on the loss of her home. She retorted by stating, "I need it no longer anyway. For the narrow house will soon be my home and you wretches cannot burn that. But you! Who will console you for the loss of your brig? She now carries a curse and will not sail long."

The owner scoffed at the old woman's words, for he had no doubt his ship was seaworthy and his crew among the most experienced to sail those waters. This he assured Rachel as the brig navigated past the hidden shoals and bars that had claimed so many other vessels. All the while, the old woman mumbled and chanted curses in the direction of the brig, and then in a blinding moment, she thrust her bony arm into the air and let out a scream like a banshee. The crowd focused their attention on her but was quickly drawn away by a cry from another. The brig had come to a sudden stop and shuddered before breaking up. It listed and sank until only the tops of the masts were visible above the water. Rescue crews frantically rowed out to the sunken ship, picking up the crew as they swam for their lives. All were brought to shore and accounted for, except for one—the man who dared insult Rachel and burn her home. During the mêlée, no one noticed that Rachel had died just after the ship hit the rock previously unknown to the area's navigators.

Rachel was buried on the site where her house once stood, and the rock that sent the brig to its doom was forever known as Rachel's Curse.

# JONATHAN MOULTON COULD NOT FOOL THE DEVIL

There is among the interred in the Pine Hill Cemetery of Hampton, New Hampshire, one stone that is a memorial to a lost hero. General Jonathan Moulton was not killed in battle and buried anonymously or lost at sea. He was, as unusual as it sounds, lost in his own backyard. General Moulton's story is quite fascinating; whether completely factual or not will be up to the reader to decide.

Jonathan Moulton was born in 1726 and died in 1787. His heroism was known far and wide among the colonies. He led troops at the Battle of Louisbourg in the French and Indian War, was instrumental in the British defeat at Saratoga during the American Revolution and was a dear friend of George Washington.

General Moulton was a prosperous man with a relentless savvy for business and a quick temper. He, his wife Abigail and their children lived in a comfortable home, but it was not enough for the general. One day, he was overheard declaring that he desired more wealth and swore he would give his soul for such riches. Within minutes, there came a knock on his door, and a man appeared in a black cloak and hat. As one might guess, it was the devil.

He approached Moulton with a proposition: his soul for all the riches he could ever wish. To prove his validity, he opened his cloak, and several gold pieces fell to the floor. Moulton quickly scooped them up and, upon close scrutiny, found them genuine in weight and size. "I will make you," said the devil, "the richest man in the province. Sign this paper, and on the first day of every month I will fill your boots with gold; but if you try any tricks with me, you will regret it. For I know you, Jonathan Moulton. Sign."

The deal was undoubtedly tempting, but the general hesitated. "Come, come, my good man. I have more appointments and must travel many leagues in several minutes. In fact, I am due at your friend the governor's home as soon as I leave here."

Moulton thought for a moment and then retorted, "Well, at least I will be in good company," as he scribbled his moniker on the contract. The devil then gave him instructions to leave a pair of boots on a crane in the fireplace at the beginning of each month, and they would be filled with gold coins. Moulton did as was requested, but before starting his routine, he went to the cobbler and had the largest pair of boots he could possibly order custom made for the deal.

And so it was that the devil kept his end of the bargain. Each month, the boots were filled to the brim with gold. Moulton became wealthy as promised, and the people of Hampton began to suspect him of making a deal with the devil, which is precisely what he did. As time went on, Moulton became obsessed with his riches and wanted more. That was when he came up with a plan. The devil showed up the next month and began pouring the gold down the chimney into the boots. No matter how much gold he poured in, they would not top off. The devil became suspicious. He peered into the window and found that Moulton had cut holes in the soles of the boots, causing the gold to pile up on the floor.

Angered by such a deed, the devil set fire to the home, burning it to the ground. The family and servants barely escaped the conflagration with their bare essentials. When the general went to retrieve the gold from the burned-out cellar hole, all that was found was a great lump of melted iron.

Memorial stone for Jonathan Moulton, the man who sold his soul to the devil.

Moulton rebuilt the mansion, but in 1774, Abigail, who had borne him eleven children, died. At fifty years of age, the general married Sarah Emery, the thirty-six-year-old friend of his recently deceased wife. On their wedding night, it was reported that Abigail, who had died of smallpox barely a year previous, appeared at the bedside of Sarah, tearing the wedding ring from her finger.

Two stories accompanied the general's death in 1787. The first was that after he was buried, his body disappeared from the coffin. It was the widespread consensus in town that the devil had taken his part of the bargain. The other story states that Moulton and his wife, Abigail, were buried in their Hampton estate garden. Shortly after, the railroads came through, and the house was moved, forever displacing the graves' exact location.

Hampton's citizens erected a memorial in his honor among the other Moulton family stones in the Pine Hill Cemetery. As for the general's actual whereabouts, only the devil may know.

# Grave Concerns

## A MACABRE MONUMENT MARKS THE SPOT OF A GRUESOME MURDER

On October 4, 1875, the small town of Pembroke, New Hampshire, was thrown into a panic when seventeen-year-old Josie Langmaid failed to show up for school at the Pembroke Academy. When her parents learned she had gone missing, they alerted neighbors who, in turn, organized a search party. About one hundred citizens from Pembroke and nearby Suncook took to the woods, scouring over two miles between her home and the school in search of the lost girl. At nine o'clock in the evening, searchers using torches for light found the body of Josie Langmaid in the woods about one-half mile from the academy. Her clothing was torn and bloody and her body mutilated. The most shocking part of the discovery was that her head had been severed from her body and could not be found.

It was not until the next morning that her head was found about one-half mile from where her body was discovered, wrapped in a bloody cape. Her face had been cut, and there was a mark on her cheek apparently caused by the heel of a shoe or boot. A broken and bloodstained club was found on a nearby road. Later examination determined that she was raped. Her remains were laid to rest in the family plot in Buck Street Cemetery on what is now Pinewood Road.

The police suspected several persons, but their first serious suspect was a man named William Drew. Drew lived close by the Langmaids in a small

Josie Langmaid monument, Pembroke, New Hampshire.

shack with his wife. He was known to be loose with his tongue regarding remarks made toward women. Drew tried to flee but was caught and arrested. One of Josie Langmaid's teachers came forth and told the police Josie had a run-in with Drew and threatened to tell her father after he threw insults at her. Drew reportedly responded by telling Josie he would cut her into little pieces if she dared speak of the incident.

A friend of Drew's, Charles Moody, was also arrested as an alleged accessory to the crime. It seemed the police had suspects, but it was not until several days later that a wire sent from St. Albans, Vermont, informed officials a similar murder had taken place in their town. A man named Joseph Lapage was arrested for the crime but released due to insufficient evidence. Lapage had moved to Suncook with his wife and four children. The police, having investigated all of Drew's and Moody's alibis, had no choice but to release them for lack of evidence. They then turned their suspicions to Lapage.

On October 13, 1875, Lapage was arrested after authorities searched his home and found a bloodstained coat and a boot heel that matched the mark on Josie's face. Lapage was tried twice for the crime and was eventually found guilty. On the day of his execution, Lapage confessed to both murders and drew a map of where he had hidden Josie's possessions. Authorities followed the route and found the missing possessions. Lapage was hanged on March 15, 1878.

The town erected a monument near the spot where her body was found. The fifteen-foot-tall obelisk sits on Academy Road across the street from Three Rivers School. One side reads: "Erected by the citizens of Pembroke and vicinity to commemorate the place of the tragic death and memory of Josie A. Langmaid, a student of the Pembroke Academy who was murdered on her way to school on October 4, 1875, AE 17 yrs 10 mos 27 days."

Another side reads: "Death lie on her like an untimely frost upon the sweetest flow'r of all the field." The third side contains the most grisly inscription: "Body found 90 ft north at stone hub. Head found 82 rods north at stone hub."

Small granite posts mark the places where her body and head were found. If one follows the directions correctly, they will arrive at the markers. One may even witness the ghostly re-creation of the murder or the ghosts of the search party that discovered the gruesome act that took place over 140 years ago. There is a video that claims to show the ghost of Lapage quickly appearing and then vanishing in a mist as a train passes by. Whether it is just smoke from the train, dust trailing the last car or a real

*Above*: The marker in the woods where Josie Langmaid's body was discovered.

*Left*: Dedication plaque on the Josie Langmaid monument.

ghost is a matter of conjecture. What is certain is it seems peculiar that the town chose to remember Josie Langmaid the way she was found in death and not the way she was in life.

## Lucas Douglass

On December 5, 1895, seventy-two-year-old Lucas Douglass was found dead on a snow-laden street in Ashford, Connecticut. He died alone, cold and penniless, having never married, and had few relatives to share time with. He was buried in the Westford Hill Cemetery, a small village burial ground. His burial plot is easy to find because it is the largest in the diminutive graveyard. The "pauper's" grave is adorned with a 34-foot-tall white Italian marble monument complete with separate headstone surrounded by a 140-foot stone fence. Large urns adorn each corner of the wall and entrance. There is also a large walkway flanked by two rows of hedges leading to the grave.

The first thought that comes to mind is, how could this be? How could a man who died penniless on the streets afford such a magnificent monument worthy of any royalty? It seems that Mr. Douglass was very frugal during

The Lucas Douglass monument in Ashford, Connecticut.

One of the many ornate carvings on Lucas Douglass's thirty-four-foot monument.

his life, saving just about every penny he earned. Shortly after death, his will revealed specific instructions to erect a glorious memorial costing many thousands of dollars over his grave. The ornate structure is meticulously carved with columns and dentil work topped by a great urn. One side of the monument reads, "Be Thou Faithful Unto Death."

Underneath is written, "Lucas Douglass, Born October 28, 1823, Died December 5, 1895, Aged 72 Years." Above the inscriptions is a bas-relief of Douglass. Another side has the letters "HIS" with the sentence below, "This World Is Not My Home."

A lower section reads, "Found Dead—Dead and Alone on a Pillow of Snow in a Roofless Street. Nobody Heard His Last Faint Moan or Knew When His Sad Heart Ceased to Beat."

Above, the numbers 1896 are intertwined with each other. Another side has the epitaph, "Tho in Paths of Death I Tread, with Gloomy Horrors Overspread, My Steadfast Heart Shall Fear No Ill, for Thou O Lord Art with Me Still. Thy Friendly Crook Shall Give Me Aid, and Guide Me Through the Dreadful Shade."

The upper section is adorned with the alpha-omega symbol, which is Greek for the beginning and end. Other such inscriptions as "I Have Heard Thy Call" and "Death Is But a Gentle Slumber" ornament the memorial.

Douglass selected the design, inscriptions and symbols long before he breathed his last breath. All but perhaps the inscription describing his death was his original design. This may have been an unfinished script waiting for the final moment of his life. Either way, Lucas Douglass, who passed through and from this life, mostly unnoticed, knew that the last vestige of eternity would lie in the grave marker that would cover his mortal remains. Each year, hundreds of tourists travel the small country roads of Ashford to get a glimpse of the man who "died penniless" but was buried in a plot fit for a king.

# WARREN GIBBS

Warren Gibbs lived a rather typical life for the times. His fame in the annals of New England came after his death and the subsequent marker he received to point out the spot of his eternal repose—and point a finger as to who may have perpetrated his demise.

In the early spring of 1860, Warren Gibbs became very ill. At first, friends and family shrugged off his symptoms—a burning throat and a dire thirst—as nothing more than a spring cold or flu. Neighbors brought cider for him to drink, which made him feel somewhat better. His wife, Mary, prepared a meal of oysters for the recovering man. After consuming the oysters, the burning and thirst returned. Despite all aid from his family and neighbors, Warren Gibbs grew increasingly ill until he died a few days later. He was laid to rest in the Pelham, Massachusetts Knights Corner Burial Ground.

Warren's brother William suspected that something was amiss. He questioned how his strong and healthy brother could succumb to a strange and accelerated illness in just days. He came to the conclusion that Warren's wife had mixed arsenic with the oyster stew and nefariously served it to Warren. In fact, William went to the authorities about his suspicion of Mary. The authorities did not have enough evidence to warrant an autopsy and dismissed the claim, but William was so convinced that the wife murdered his brother that he decided to make a public declaration. This was achieved by having his accusation literally carved in stone. The stone was Warren's headstone. The monument reads:

> *Warren Gibbs—Died by Arsenic Poison—March 23, 1860—Age 36 years five mos 23 days. Think my friends when this you see—How my wife has dealt by me—She in some oysters did prepare—Some poison for my lot and share—Then of the same I did partake—And nature yielded to its fate—Before she my wife became—Mary Felton was her name. Erected by his brother—Wm Gibbs.*

Mary's family, naturally outraged by this act of accusation, removed the stone from the plot. In retaliation, William put the stone back and threatened

Warren Gibbs's stone in Pelham, Massachusetts.

legal action if they were to touch it again. Legend has it he also put a curse on the stone to forestall any further vandalism to Warren's final resting place. The story of Warren Gibbs became known far and wide, and his widow, although never formally charged, was forever under the suspicious eye of the Gibbs family.

The stone stood untouched for the rest of the family's mortal years. Later, it needed to be replaced when "modern" legend-trippers began to vandalize the marker. The original tombstone was housed safely in the Pelham Historical Society Museum. There are claims that the headstone in the museum is not original either. There are tales told of the stone being stolen, only to be mysteriously returned because of the impending curse. The stone vanished again in 1940 only to be rediscovered in 1947. It rested untouched for seven years in the basement of a farmhouse in nearby Palmer. Since then, the stone in the Knights Cemetery has rested peacefully in the far right corner of the burying ground. Whether Warren and his brother do is another story.

## THE HILLERS' MONUMENTAL MONUMENT

The town of Wilmington, Massachusetts, in 1870 boasted a whopping 866 residents. Over the years, this would change as more people decided that the locale was the perfect small town to plant their family roots. One such person was Dr. Henry Hiller, who, along with his wife, France, honeymooned in America before deciding it would be the perfect place to practice medicine.

Henry's wife was also a medical doctor, and the two became wealthy in their practices. The couple met in London, England, and were married in 1868, choosing Cape Cod for their honeymoon destination. Henry invented and patented an elixir he sold at his Tremont Street location in Boston. The money flowed in, but the one thing they really longed for was to have children. Of the twenty-three children whom France bore, fourteen were twins; however, all of them died very early in life, leaving the couple childless.

The Hillers were among the millions who were caught up in the Spiritualist movement of the nineteenth and early twentieth centuries. They felt there was some sort of afterlife, and when it came their time, they wanted to greet it in something more elaborate than a pine box. That was when they came up with a "monumental" idea.

The couple hired James McGregor, a renowned woodcarver of the time, to carry out their plan. The Hillers were to have two gargantuan caskets with inner boxes constructed and carved with specific figures and other ornamentation. After going over the specifications, McGregor informed them it would take about seven years to complete the caskets. At a promise of forty dollars a day, a good sum back then, McGregor and his apprentices went to work on the caskets.

On November 7, 1888, Henry Hiller died at age forty-three after a carriage accident. A few weeks before he died, one of his neighbors inquired as to the status of the caskets. Hiller replied, "Oh, it will be ready when I need it." Unfortunately, the casket was not ready, and Dr. Hiller's body was placed in a vault for ten months.

On September 1, 1889, the first casket was completed, and the construction of the second one commenced. Henry's funeral was held a few days later, and his magnificent casket was placed in a specially designed unfinished mausoleum intended to be forty feet square by forty feet high with plate-glass windows protected by bronze grating, allowing visitors to look in and behold the breathtaking enclosures of repose. Each morning, France would visit the tomb to say good morning to Henry and put fresh flowers on his grave.

Three and a half years later, the second casket, an exact duplicate of the first, was delivered to Mrs. Hiller's door. The outside was supported by eight seventeen-inch-tall brass lion's paws. The casket had two ivory vines running along its outer edge, converging in the center at a carved skull with a lizard coming out of one of its eye sockets. On the side of the box were angels, cupids, bats flying over serpents and dragons carved in an array of places. One of the more eclectic designs was a large owl holding a field mouse in its talons.

The inner box held a steel hammock suspended from four corners of the chamber. The cover of this box contained gold- and silver-plated plaques with the names and portraits of the couple and their twenty-three children. In all, each casket stood five feet from the floor, weighed a little over a ton and cost $30,000 to build. Initially, expensive redwood was ordered for their construction, but it was discarded for a more expensive cedar. The cedar would be replaced by a more "choice" wood: mahogany.

Mrs. Hiller was extremely proud of her casket and displayed it for all to see. When friends came by, she would don her white satin burial gown with over five hundred yards of lace. Her attendants would place her in a satin hammock and lower it into the coffin just to show how wonderful her appearance would be when laid out. A mirror on the ceiling gave France a bird's-eye view of how she would look at her own funeral. After a while, she had a wax model of herself cast, dressed it in her burial robes and laid that into the casket. At one point, she put the casket on exhibit at Boston's Horticultural Hall. She became known as the "Lady of the Caskets."

Five years after Mr. Hiller died, Mrs. Hiller remarried. The invitations stated the recipient was cordially invited to the renewal of the marriage vows of Mrs. France Hiller and Mr. Henry Hiller on Easter Sunday, April 2, 1893. This invitation caused quite a confusion among the townsfolk, but it soon came to light that Mrs. Hiller had fallen for her coachman, Peter Surrette. He had wooed her, and she was flattered by his faithfulness, gentlemanly qualities and the admiration he held for her. Mrs. Hiller accepted his proposal, but first, she required that he legally change his name to Henry Hiller. He not only complied with her request but kept this name for the rest of his life.

Mrs. Hiller died on May 18, 1900, at the age of fifty-six. The day of the funeral was a grandiose affair. Workmen wheeled the casket from the small granite building where it was stored onto the lawn. A special lifting device brought in from Boston loaded the great sarcophagus onto the bed of a specially designed funeral car, and off to the cemetery they went. Thousands turned out for a glimpse of the massive coffin as it made its final journey to the Hiller mausoleum.

Ten of the strongest men in the town were hired to lift the casket off the truck and onto the veranda railings. The railings immediately buckled under its weight. Bearers quickly scrambled to support the casket and center it on the car, which, including the canopy, reached a height of almost nineteen feet. The height of car and coffin was too tall to pass under the trolley wires, so carpenters were called in to cut fourteen inches off the posts of the funeral truck's canopy. The procession to the burial ground was a somber affair. The streets were lined with reporters and onlookers. The churchyard was packed with people hoping to get a glimpse of the majestic coffin. It was the funeral of a lifetime.

The service was held, and the sarcophagus was rolled into the mausoleum alongside the first Henry Hiller to remain for eternity. Eternity, however, was not as long as the Hillers expected. The great mausoleum was never

*Left*: Funeral procession for Mrs. Hiller. *Courtesy of the Wilmington Historical Society.*

*Below*: France Hiller's great sarcophagus being transported to its final resting place. *Courtesy of the Wilmington Historical Society.*

actually completed to original specifications. In June 1935, the tomb had become run-down and began leaking. Henry Hiller #2 decided it best to have it razed and the coffins buried. The coffins were taken from the tomb and buried with two small stone urns over each one, creating a very humble end for such an extravagant saga.

As for Henry Hiller #2, he survived France by fifty-eight years, dying at the age of eighty-nine. He remained unmarried and lived in the Hiller home for most of his life until moving in with his family in later years. The two small urns still mark the final resting place of the Hillers, whose incredible creations designed to eternally house their bones now lie unseen moldering beneath the soil.

# The Strange Premonition of Francis Lightfoot Eddy

A few miles north of Rutland, Vermont, in a wooded valley sheltered by the slopes of the beautiful Green Mountains, is the tiny hamlet of Chittenden. On a quiet back road sits a large, remodeled nineteenth-century farmhouse. The building is presently a ski lodge owned by the High Life Ski Club, but it was once the center of communication with the spirit universe.

An attorney and former Civil War colonel, Henry Steel Olcott (August 2, 1832–February 17, 1907), while writing for the *New York Sun*, paid a ten-week visit to the Eddy family to find out once and for all if what he had heard was actually true. Allegedly, the members of the Eddy family possessed an incredible supernatural ability to summon the dead. The Spiritualist movement was at its height around 1874, and there were many who claimed to have the same uncanny powers that defied logic and reason. Very few, if any, would leave a lasting impression on those who witnessed these "acts" of mediumship, such as the Eddy family claimed to possess. Olcott later published his experience with the Eddy family in his book *People from the Other World* in 1874, giving a complete perspective of what happened at the Eddy homestead before and during his tenure there.

Zephaniah Eddy and his wife, Julia Ann MacCombs, had eleven known children: John Westley (born in 1832), William H. (1832–October 25, 1932), Francis Lightfoot (1834–March 18, 1862), Maranda D. (1836–March 29, 1871), Sophia Jane (February 2, 1840–July 18, 1913), Horatio G. (1842–September 8, 1922), Mary C. (April 1, 1844–December 31, 1910), James H. (1846–April 18, 1862), Delia M. (1849–January 28, 1922, although her stone states her birth date as 1853), Daniel Webster (September 17, 1852–September 6, 1926) and Alice Julia (April 2, 1857–April 20, 1887).

All of the children exhibited strange powers to one extent or another that defied rational explanation. The Eddy children inherited the ability of mediumship from their mother's ancestry. Their mother, Julia, came from a long line of mediums and psychics. Her great-great-grandmother Mary Perkins Bradbury was tried, convicted and sentenced to hang on September 22, 1692, for witchcraft during the Salem witch hysteria. Somehow, perhaps due to a bribe to the jailer or a daring escape, she managed to gain freedom and flee to Amesbury, Massachusetts. After the hysteria had dwindled, she removed to Salisbury, Massachusetts, where she died on December 20, 1700.

Although several of the family members made their talents widely known, one incident stood out in the brief life of Francis Lightfoot Eddy, who served

The Eddy home in Chittenden, Vermont, once known as the "Spirit Capital of the Universe."

as orderly sergeant of Company G, Fifth Vermont Volunteers, during the Civil War. The Fifth Regiment was composed of members from St. Albans, Middlebury, Swanton, Hyde Park, Manchester, Cornwall, Rutland, Brandon, Burlington, Poultney, Tinmouth and Richmond.

Francis enlisted on August 21, 1861. During his tenure with the regiment, he became ill with a simple cold. This cold eventually turned into running consumption (tuberculosis), thus sealing his fate. Francis was discharged due to his disability on December 14, 1861.

During his hospice, Francis penned an eerie notation in the family Bible stating the exact time and date he would die. Shortly before his death, the sound of a wagon came to a halt in front of the Eddys' door. The family then heard some scuffling, and the front door burst open, revealing two soldiers carrying a coffin with a brass nameplate on the lid. The soldiers uttered not a single sound as they solemnly lowered the coffin to the floor and exited. When the family peered through the glass panes, the wagon and its passengers had mysteriously vanished into thin air.

The dim light of the hallway proved too difficult to read the name on the brass plate. The family quickly dispatched in search of a candle to illuminate the room. Upon returning, the coffin had vanished. Francis, at the young age

*Above*: The Eddy family burial lot in Chittenden, Vermont.

*Right*: The grave of Francis Lightfoot Eddy.

of twenty-eight, passed on to the other side at the exact date and time he previously scribed in the family Bible, March 18, 1862. The family ordered a coffin from nearby Rutland. When the coffin was delivered, the Eddys were astounded by what they beheld. The casket was the exact one that the ghostly soldiers had brought a short time before, complete with the same brass nameplate. This time, however, the soldiers were living flesh and blood duplicates of the previous spectral ones. Francis was laid to rest in the Baird Cemetery, a short distance from the former Eddy home.

"Passed into the world of spirits." This verse, or a slight variation of it, would become a common inscription on several of the Eddy gravestones. "Entered the world of spirits" is inscribed on Julia and Maranda's stone, who died in 1871 and 1872, respectively. "Passed to spirit life" can be found on the monuments of William, Horatio, Alice and a few others who were immediate relations of the family. Incidentally, Francis's brother James died exactly one month after Francis on April 18. Their father followed them on July 13 of the same year.

As for the soldiers, they twice showed their faces at the home. Who they were is lost to antiquity. We only know they came to deliver the strange omen of death to the Eddy door, as was common before a member of the Eddy family was to pass into the world of spirits.

# John P. Bowman's Eternal Pose

Route 103 in Cuttingsville, Vermont, is emblematic when it comes to small-town New England thoroughfares. The landscape is truly rural and picturesque, with farmhouses and fields dotting the landscape. But at one point, an eerie sight looms over the road just beyond the wall that encompasses the Laurel Glen Cemetery, causing the unwary traveler to give a second glance at the structure in the burial ground. A white figure can be seen leaning against the wall of an impressive tomb that casts a somber shadow over the small road. No, it is not a ghost but rather the mournful statue of a man crouching alongside the door of the Laurel Glen Mausoleum with a wreath in one hand and a key in the other. It is the stone figure of Clarendon, Vermont native John Porter Bowman, a wealthy farmer and tanning tycoon.

Since 1881, travelers have beheld the statue that graced the steps of the vault ten years before Bowman passed away. The design of the crypt and lifelike sculpture was Bowman's own creation. The project called for

The statue of John Porter Bowman awaiting at the door of the family mausoleum with key and wreath in hand. *Courtesy of Vickie and Bob Hughes.*

125 masons and sculptors working a little over a year to complete. Inside, the remains of the Bowman family lie in repose, complete with a stone bust of both his wife, Jennie, and daughter Ella, who died tragically and mysteriously within several months of each other. A life-size statue of his first daughter Addie, who died as an infant, stands on one side, and the bust of Mr. Bowman looks over them in eternal love and devotion. The mausoleum is open during the warmer months, so the curious may glimpse inside and see the spectacular interior of the small burial vault. The busts can be seen from all sides with the aid of mirrors placed on the walls, creating an illusion of the chamber appearing much larger than it actually is. The tile floor and other accoutrements are also meticulously laid out. Just beholding the creation makes the trek worthy of any legend tripper. In fact, many have made this site a destination point during their visit to the Green Mountain State.

Across the road from the cemetery is the home that Bowman had built for his family. Their first child Addie died in 1854, an infant at the time of her death. Ella was twenty-two years old when she passed away in 1879. His wife, Jennie, followed shortly after in 1880. Within the course of one year, Bowman became a widower without children.

Close-up of the statue peering inside the tomb. *Courtesy of Vickie and Bob Hughes.*

Bowman survived ten years of solemn grief before joining his family on the other side in 1891 at age seventy-five. Before he passed away, he set up a trust fund for the perpetual upkeep of the mansion and grounds. Being an ardent believer in reincarnation, he wanted the mansion to be in "waiting readiness" when he and his family returned. The custodian of the property kept the clocks wound, lights lit and a warm fire in the hearth in expectation of their return. It never happened, and the funds were depleted by 1953. The mansion became a rental property, but tenants fled the home, stating the Bowmans were in fact living there again. In time, the mansion was closed and secured by the Laurel Glen Cemetery Association. Odd noises and strange lights are heard and seen around the now-closed mansion and mausoleum. Perhaps the spirits of the family cross the road every night to visit the spacious home that temporarily housed them in life before returning to the small vault that eternally houses them in death.

# Dr. Timothy Clark Smith

The old saying "the doctor knows best" just may apply in this story of a New Haven, Vermont physician obsessed with the fear of being buried alive. Taphophobia, the fear of being buried alive, led Dr. Timothy Clark Smith to design the construction of a special burial vault—a tomb with a view.

Smith was born on June 14, 1821, in Monktin, Vermont, and received his bachelor's degree from Middlebury College in 1842 and a medical degree from University of the City of New York in 1855. His illustrious career took him the world over, and somewhere along the way, he developed his crippling fear of premature burial.

Dr. Smith was not alone in his grave concern. In the eighteenth and nineteenth centuries, thousands of people were buried or almost buried alive. There were countless reports of the sick or dying experiencing what became known as Lazarus Syndrome, a condition where the body spontaneously automatically resuscitates itself after all signs of life are allegedly extinguished. Today, thanks to medical science, the event is extremely rare, but back in Dr. Clark's day, exhumed coffins would often reveal horrific signs of the supposedly dead person waking up and trying to claw their way out of their casket.

Bells were placed above ground with a string attached to the corpse's wrist. Wakes became a common event for fear the "dead" may not actually be dead. Various inventions were touted with claims that a premature burial could be discovered and remedied, but the only drawback was someone would have to be present when the interred woke from their condition.

To solve this dilemma, people were often hired to watch the grave for several days in wait of the bell to ring or whatever contraption was put in place, alarming the vigilant that the person below was not dead. The good doctor took his invention many steps further to ensure a safe awakening.

Dr. Clark married Catherine Jane Prout, and they had four children together, all living well into adulthood. Smith died on February 25, 1893, in Middlebury, Vermont, but before he passed, he had prepared the peculiar crypt for he and his wife.

The special grave site was designed below a mound that contained a crypt for Smith with another chamber below for his wife. A cement tube led from where his face would be positioned to the surface of the mound. A fourteen-by-fourteen-inch window was placed at the top of the tube so the doctor could see above if he woke. He was also buried with a special bell in his hand so he could signal for help. As far as anyone knows, the good doctor never awoke from his eternal slumber. The window is still there for people to peer in, but moss and condensation have made it almost impossible to see into the crypt. It is more than likely that the doctor cannot see out as well.

## Asa "Popcorn" Snow

Dana, along the shores of the Quabbin Reservoir in Massachusetts, is home to the original tomb of Asa "Popcorn" Snow. Gate 40 on Route 32A is marked with a sign set back from the road a bit. Just right of the entrance gate, before the old road, is the old homestead and tomb of Asa "Popcorn" Snow.

Asa Snow was born on Cape Cod in the 1790s. In 1840, he moved to Dana. Asa Snow was a vegetarian whose diet consisted largely of milk and popcorn. Asa's first wife, Isabelle, committed suicide in 1844 by hanging herself from a piece of her dress in the barn. She was buried in the family cemetery at the edge of the farm. His daughter died a year later, and he buried her next to Isabelle.

In the late 1860s, Asa decided to build a family vault to house his loved ones and, eventually, his own remains. Before moving his first wife to the crypt, and much to his second wife's protest, he displayed her remains for friends and neighbors to view. For what particular reason is now lost to antiquity.

Soon after, he began to build a metal coffin with a glass top for his own burial. Snow also made arrangements for the local undertaker to spend seven days watching over the coffin, in case Asa suddenly woke up.

In an ironic twist of fate, Asa, a devout vegetarian, died on November 29, 1872, while dragging a pig carcass into the house for his Thanksgiving dinner guests. As per agreement, the undertaker looked in on Snow, but for only three days. Snow's second wife, Eunice, relieved him of his duties, feeling that if Asa did not wake up after three days, surely the cold would have finished him off.

The peculiar sarcophagus attracted the attention of people from all over. Many flocked to get a glimpse of the well-preserved body of Popcorn Snow through the glass window of his coffin. A newspaper story from 1912 told of how Snow's body looked as fresh as it had when he died forty years earlier. His hair still shone with the luster of the living, and his clothes showed no signs of age or deterioration. Resting on top of his coffin was an old box containing the remains of his first wife and daughter. Legend has it that someone stole the teeth from Isabella's skull for use as decoration on a timepiece.

Local papers later reported that Snow's ghost would leave his tomb every year on the anniversary of his death and travel to the former site of his wife's

The relocated grave of Asa "Popcorn" Snow.

grave. The glowing apparition could be seen floating among the ruins of the old homestead before returning to his mausoleum until the next fall brought another awakening from his eternal repose.

This story prompted two men from Boston to make a bet with each other where one of them would spend a night in the tomb, waiting for the ghost to appear. The brave doubter arrived just after dark. Hitching his horse to a graveyard post, he settled into the crypt for a night he would never forget. Not long after he began his watch, his horse began whinnying and broke free from its hitch, sprinting from the scene. The man promptly exited the tomb, fleeing in fear. Although he was paid for the bet, he never came within miles of the area again.

Shortly after that incident, vandals broke the glass of the coffin, causing Asa Snow's remains to rapidly wither. Local authorities sealed the tomb from other legend trippers, and it remained that way until 1944, when the Metropolitan Water Commission relocated the bodies and leveled the farm. Snow and his family are now buried in the Quabbin Cemetery. Whether he still rises and haunts his old homestead is not known, but perhaps someone will find out, whether they mean to or not.

## THE CONFEDERATE BURIED IN A YANKEE CEMETERY

As the train solemnly came to a halt, the Colley family of Gray, Maine, stood sadly awaiting the arrival of their son, Lieutenant Charles H. Colley, of the Tenth Maine Infantry Regiment. He was not getting off the train to greet them, but rather, his casket was to be carried off for burial. Lieutenant Colley enlisted in the regiment on October 4, 1861.

The recently promoted second lieutenant received a bullet wound to the knee at the Battle of Cedar Mountain in Culpeper, Virginia, on August 9, 1862. Twenty-nine-year-old Colley succumbed to his wound on September 20, 1862, when septicemia—a bacteria in the blood that occurs in severe infections—set in. Colley's mother agreed to have the body embalmed and shipped from the hospital in Washington, D.C., to Gray for burial in the family plot.

The casket was brought forth, and the parents opened it to take one final look at their beloved fallen son and soldier. Their sadness turned to horror when they lifted the lid and gazed upon the body of a strange man wearing a Confederate uniform lying in the box in place of their son.

Grave of the unknown Confederate in Gray, Maine.

Not knowing what to do and fearful that Lieutenant Colley may have been buried and forgotten, perhaps in some field, the Colley family became worried that they would never give their son a proper burial. Many of Gray's women had lost their sons or husbands to the war, which made them think of the mother who could be waiting for her son in the Southern states.

The women of Gray collected money to give the stranger a proper burial despite the strict hatred and agony the war had brought. He was buried with honors in Gray Village Cemetery with a simple headstone that reads, "Stranger. A soldier of the late war. Died 1862. Erected by the Ladies of Gray." Every Memorial Day, the women of Gray would put a Confederate flag on the grave in respect for the stranger who was never given a name.

In another twist of fate, the Colley family petitioned the army to send them the correct body, but when it arrived, this time they trusted all was right and did not open the coffin before burying it in the family plot. The headstone for Charles H. Colley bears the inscription, "Among the first to rally in defense of his country."

He may have well been suited to honor that inscription, but whoever is buried under that stone may not have been. According to War Department records, Charles H. Colley is buried in a cemetery in Alexandria, Virginia, the soldiers' burial ground that preceded Arlington.

So, then, who is actually buried in Charles H. Colley's plot in Gray?

# DEACON WHEELOCK'S PROTECTED GRAVE

This next account comes out of Cavendish, Vermont. Although many of the facts may be common for any small-town history, the second part of this narrative, meticulously uncovered by research, really makes for a New

England tale that one may take some time to digest and then perhaps talk about for years to come.

Historians Linda Welch and Margaret Caulfield are well versed in the history of the Wheelock family. Welch published a few books for the Cavendish Historical Society that are quite absorbing and thorough. The book *Families of Cavendish* tells a bit more of the story. Whether the next account is a product of legend or fact is up to the reader to decide.

Jotham Wheelock was born to Deacon Jonathan and Anna Drury Wheelock on August 26, 1763, in Shrewsbury, Massachusetts. Jotham, like his father, served in the American Revolution, entering in 1781 at the age of eighteen as a private. In 1789, Deacon and his family moved to Cavendish.

According to town records and the historical society's book called *Heritage and Homes of Cavendish*, in 1793, Jonathan divided his property, 1,038 acres in total, among his children, leaving a small plot for his own home. It is listed in the book as the Saunders Farm. According to Margaret Caulfield, the farm was owned by a number of people over the years.

Jotham was stricken with a disease or head injury during his service in the Revolutionary War. The event left him mentally unstable. When Deacon Wheelock died in 1798, records do not indicate Jotham as being mentioned in his will, perhaps due to his condition.

Over the course of time, the illness worsened to the point where his family had to take care of him using the pension he received from his military service. Guardianship was drawn up for him in 1817 and 1831. These are on file in volume 3 of the Windsor County Probate Office. The index lists him as "insane." Perhaps he was, for his next decision was quite unusual.

Before he died, he made a strange request. Jotham strongly demanded that before he be buried and his grave filled in, a heavy plank filled with long spikes was to be placed just above his coffin. He was afraid that the devil would rob the grave of his corpse and carry him to hell.

Jotham died in Cavendish on April 27, 1831. He was buried as requested on the

Reverend Wheelock's grave in Cavendish, Vermont. *Courtesy of Vickie and Bob Hughes.*

old Saunders Farm at the upper end of the Town-Farm Road. His is the only grave in the small plot about halfway between two farms. Colonel Wilgus, a descendant of the Wheelocks, had a granite marker set at the grave site—a grave with spikes to protect him from the ravages of the devil. Truth is often stranger than fiction.

# CAROLINE CUTTER

*Murdered by the Baptist Ministry of Baptist Church as follows: September 28, 1838, Ae 33, She was accused of Lying in Church Meeting by the Rev. D.D. Pratt of Deacon Albert Adams. Was condemned by the church unheard. She was reduced to poverty by Deacon William Wallace. When an exparte council was asked of the Milford Baptist Church by the advice of their committee, George Raymond, Calvin Averill and Andrew Hutchinson, they voted not to receive any communication upon the subject: The Rev. Mark Carpenter said he thought as the good old Dear Pearson said, "we have got Cutter down and it is best to keep him down." The intentional and malicious destruction of her character and happiness as above described destroyed her life. Her last words were, "tell the truth."*

This is the inscription on the gravestone of Caroline Cutter of Milford, New Hampshire, as written by her husband, Dr. Calvin Cutter. The accounts that follow tell the tale of how Dr. Cutter became convinced the Baptist Church was responsible for the death of his wife and made sure the story would forever be told.

Dr. Calvin Cutter became a famous doctor of the times, authoring a book called *Cutter's Physiology*, which sold over several hundred thousand copies. He traveled the country lecturing on new techniques and breakthroughs in the medical field. He also served in the Civil War as a field surgeon and was at one point shot by the enemy. He escaped death's grip when the bullet miraculously deflected off his belt buckle. Cutter was a staunch abolitionist, speaking dearly of the cause. His only child, Carrie, reportedly became the first woman casualty of the Civil War while serving in the medical sector for the Union. But this would all transpire long after his claims the Baptist Church killed his wife and ruined his life.

In 1835, Nashua, New Hampshire, began planning a second Baptist church to contain the growing number of people coming into the region. Dr. Calvin Cutter was all for a new church and eagerly put up funds for its construction. According to his pamphlet, *Murder of Caroline H. Cutter by the Baptist Ministers and Baptist Churches*, Cutter was asked by the minister, Reverend Dura D. Pratt, and other church members for money to pay their shares in the church, with a promise to pay it all back within a year.

A year went by, and the members refused to pay the money back, stating they never made such a promise. Cutter's financial loss was deep. His property was seized to pay the loans he took for the church on good faith. The church soon folded and was sold for a portion of its worth to a Methodist congregation.

Cutter and his wife demanded an investigation into the matter, claiming the reverend had purchased the stock at a deep discount and then turned around and sold it for full price to mill girls in the area. Caroline Cutter confronted the Milford Baptist officials, alleging Pratt had borrowed money under false pretenses and profited from it at the loss of the church. In the meantime, Pratt and his members accused Caroline of lying in church when she read the charges of their owing money for the outstanding shares.

The Milford church refused to hear their case and even admonished the couple for their accusations and disrespect of the church. They were, of course, excommunicated. One deacon went as far as saying, "They got Cutter down. Best to keep him down."

The stress of the situation became too much for Caroline. Broken in life, mind and spirit, she passed away on September 18, 1841, at thirty-three years of age. Dr. Cutter emphasized in his pamphlet that the Baptist society "intentionally and maliciously destroyed her character and standing in the church and society." He also concluded they destroyed her peace of mind, health, happiness and well-being. He further went on to write, "As their acts were deliberate and malicious, pursued without mitigation or relaxation while she lived, it is as clearly a case of murder as if they had given arsenic to effect their purposes."

## PERSECUTED FOR WEARING A BEARD

Imagine being ostracized by a whole community because you chose to wear a beard. That is exactly what happened to Joseph Palmer of Notown, Massachusetts. Palmer, a veteran of the War of 1812, settled down to become a farmer in the small town of Notown outside of Fitchburg. Life would have been easy for him had he not chosen to become a fashion criminal of the times.

Grave of Joseph Palmer from Leominster, who was persecuted for wearing a beard.

After the 1820s, the thought of wearing a long beard was not only out of vogue, but it was sinful in the eyes of the pious. Palmer, the only citizen in the area to wear such facial hair, was openly insulted, pelted with rocks and even had his windows broken by his neighbors for sporting a long beard. The church had excommunicated him and basically called him a subject of the dark one due to his insistence on keeping his wispy whiskers. A minister told him he looked like the devil, and he replied, "Mr. Trask, are you not mistaken in your comparison of personages? I have never seen a picture of the ruler of the sulfurous regions with much of a beard, but if I remember correctly, Jesus wore a beard not unlike mine."

Close-up of Palmer's monument shows a bas-relief of his fashion choice carved into his stone.

In 1830, Palmer was leaving the Old Fitchburg Hotel on business when he was approached by four men who accosted him with scissors and a knife in an attempt to shave him. The two-hundred-pound Palmer managed to stab two of the aggressors in the leg with his pocketknife before emerging from the scramble unscathed and unshaven.

Palmer was arrested for the attack and fined. Although he had the funds to pay his fine, he refused and was thrown in jail for fifteen months. Even in prison he was not safe, as he was met with the same attacks twice by both inmates and guards. In the meantime, word got out of the incident, making the people of Fitchburg look deplorable in the public eye. The sheriff decided to release Palmer and drop any charges, but the bearded man refused unless a proclamation was made where he could wear his beard and walk the streets in safety and comfort. This never happened, and Palmer, refusing to leave the jail, was finally tied to a chair and literally thrown into the street.

Palmer later achieved celebrity status for his crusade for freedom of individual facial hair choice, as well as becoming an avid abolitionist and temperance supporter. He became friends with several authors including Emerson and Thoreau. Louisa May Alcott's *Transcendental Wild Oats* features him as the character Moses White.

Joseph Palmer died on October 30, 1873, at the age of eighty-four. He was buried in the Evergreen Cemetery in Leominster, Massachusetts, with a stone bearing his likeness sporting, of course, his long beard. On the stone, the epitaph reads, "Persecuted for Wearing the Beard."

# THE STRANGE BURIAL IN DAMARISCOTTA, MAINE

The Howe family of New England were among the first settlers in the New World. The family grew and spread to different areas of the region, becoming an important part of New England's fabric in one way or another. In Damariscotta, Maine, one branch of the family made history in a more macabre fashion. Here is their story.

Colonel Joel Howe, born in Worcester, Massachusetts, in 1748, married Mary Gates in 1770. After the War of 1812, he, his wife and their family of nine children moved to Damariscotta, purchasing a plot of land where Elm and Hodgdon Streets now exist. After the Colonel died, the family moved across the street and established Howe's Tavern. Joel III became the proprietor, and business boomed. Many distinguished guests such as President James K. Polk made the tavern a destination for refreshment and drink.

The Howe family soon became caught up in the Spiritualist movement that swept the nation in the nineteenth century. Edwin and Lorenzo were somewhat interested in the movement, but their sister Mary became most fascinated with the idea of walking between two worlds. She became a medium and held séances at the tavern, falling into trances, sometimes for days without stirring a muscle. People flocked from miles around to witness Mary's uncanny ability.

During a séance, a woman asked Mary when a relative would return from his visit to New York City. Mary began mumbling and uttering that she saw many lights and feared he would not return. "When all those lights appear, he will die!" She exclaimed.

Several days later, news came that the man died of a heart attack the exact same moment the new gas lights were turned on to illuminate the Brooklyn Bridge.

Her trances were something to behold. She would appear to be dead but in time would arise from her strange slumber with no apparent after effects. Then in 1882, Mary died—or did she?

Mary had gone into one of her trances and lay inert for the better part of a week. Edwin invited the curious in to glimpse at the phenomenon and explained that the stones were placed around the body to keep her warm. As another week passed, some of the townsfolk became suspicious and called the authorities. The constable decided to further investigate the matter, calling on Dr. Robert Dixon to examine the woman. When he arrived, Mary had no discernible pulse or noticeable breath, yet her skin was supple and full of color, her cheeks rosy and her eyes still full of life. There was no indication of rigor mortis, as she remained warm and flexible. With nothing else to go by but respiration and pulse, the attending physician declared her deceased and ordered her buried at once.

The constable, undertaker and doctor carried her away despite many protests from neighbors who knew Mary. They attested witnessing Mary go into trances for long periods before waking up like nothing had happened. Benjamin Metcalf refused to let the throng bury her in his cemetery, forcing them to make the trip to Glidden Cemetery in Newcastle. Still the deed was done, and Mary was committed to the earth.

The task was met with much difficulty, as no one would dig the grave for fear that she was being buried alive. The undertaker's assistant refused to lower the body into the grave, leaving the constable, minister and undertaker to perform the grueling task. Her grave remained unmarked for fear she would be exhumed at once.

After the burial, even the most daring of souls refused to pass the cemetery. Many claimed to witness strange lights accompanied by moans and groans coming from the earth. Dogs would abruptly stop while passing by the burying yard and howl in fear. The Howe Tavern became the Plummer House before becoming a hospital and later Clark's Apartments. The home where the incident took place was known as the George Alva Chapman House.

Was she buried alive, or did Mary Howe really meet her maker? We may never know as so much time has passed. People still claim to hear the moans from the cemetery and search for her grave. There is a circle of trees where a few stones were uprooted in more recent years. Could one of these be Mary's grave?

## Captain Samuel Jones

Captain Samuel Jones, son of Hannah Hoar and Samuel Jones, was born in Hillsboro, New Hampshire, on September 30, 1777. Samuel married Deborah Bradford, and in 1800, the couple removed to Washington, New Hampshire. According to officials, this was the first town in the United States to be named after the honorable George Washington. The town meeting of December 13, 1776, was when this memorable event took place.

While assisting in the moving of a building in 1804, the captain's left leg became caught and trapped between the foundation of the building and a fence. Unfortunately, the leg was so badly injured that it had to be amputated. There was a belief at the time that if one lost a part of their body and buried it in the proper position in a coffin that would someday tenant the rest of the person, they would be reunited in death.

Captain Jones's leg was buried with military honors in the village cemetery on Faxon Hill Road, just below the town common. A proper stone was set in place with the epitaph "Capt. Samuel Jones Leg which was amputated July 7, 1804."

Whether Captain Jones was reunited with his leg after death may never be known, for some time after, he moved to Massachusetts, Rhode Island and New York. His whereabouts are mostly unknown to this day. Some accounts claim he is buried in Boston and some say Rhode Island. Research by the author came across a grave in Schenectady, New York, with the name Samuel Jones, born 1777 and died February 13, 1849, age seventy-one years, eight months and three days. If this is the captain, then he and his leg are among the only Americans buried in two different states.

# XYZ

Even some of the most seeded folk of Big River, Connecticut, are not familiar with this next story, which at one time catapulted the sleepy little community into temporary limelight. The story goes back to Wednesday, December 13, 1899, when four men showed up in the dead of night to rob the Deep River Savings Bank. Only three would escape with their lives.

Somehow, the detectives of a New York–based bankers' association had tipped the bank off almost a year prior of a possible robbery. They either knew of the impending robbery long before or the would-be thieves took a long time to finally get to Big River to fulfill their evil plan. Either way, something had to be done, so the bank hired a local man named Captain Harry Tyler, who just happened to be a crack shot with a rifle. Tyler kept vigil guarding the bank each night in expectation of the robbers' arrival.

Then on December 13, 1899, it happened. The four men showed up in the cloak of darkness as previously informed. One man began to pry a window open for the bandits to gain access, but before he could finish the task, Captain Tyler took aim and felled him with a single shot. The other three robbers fled the scene and were never seen from in those parts again.

The body was brought to the undertaker, but a thorough search disclosed there was no identity on the deceased. There were dynamite cartridges

The stone of XYZ. Note all the offerings that have been left.

found in his suit, revealing he may have attempted to blow up the safe once inside the bank. Who he was, however, still remained a mystery to all.

With nothing else to do, the citizens of Deep River buried the man in a far corner of the Fountain Hill Cemetery in a donated plot. It was not long before Captain Tyler received a letter in a woman's handwriting requesting the young man be buried under a headstone with nothing more than the letters "XYZ" inscribed on it. This was complied with, and a small stone about the size of a modern-day electric toaster soon replaced a crude cross with the initials as requested.

The story of XYZ and the mystery surrounding who he was would have ended there, but for the next forty years or so, a woman came to town once a year to pay a visit to the grave of the unknown stranger. She would arrive by train, walk down the tracks a mile or so, enter the back of the cemetery and leave a flower at the grave of XYZ. She was always dressed in black from head to toe with a cloak covering her face from full view. No one ever confronted her, but deep down, it was implied that she was the one who requested the strange grave initials for the unfortunate thief.

It was not until the end of February 1900 that the mystery of XYZ was allegedly solved. The *New Era*, a very popular paper of the time, published that the burglar had been identified as Frank Howard, a notorious and hardened criminal with a violent record. It went on to state that detectives of the American Bankers Association had discovered he went under several other aliases such as Frank Ellis, Tom Howard and P.E. King. He was known in Michigan, New York and Massachusetts as a dangerous criminal.

The Deep River Bank is now Citizens Bank, and Captain Tyler's gun is on display at the bank he saved from being pillaged by the would-be looters. As for XYZ, many believe that his real identity is still a mystery that may never be solved.

# Unique Yankee Legends

## Handkerchief Moody

Nathaniel Hawthorne wrote a fictional short story called "The Minister's Black Veil" about a man who preached to his congregation with a black handkerchief shrouding his face. It seems Hawthorne was well versed in New England history, for such a person actually existed. Reverend Joseph Moody was a highly respected minister of the Second Church of York, Maine.

Joseph Moody was born in 1700 in York. His father, the famous Samuel Moody, was often labeled quite eccentric. Joseph graduated from Harvard University in 1718. He then took positions as a schoolmaster, county clerk and judge. In 1732, he decided to follow in his father's footsteps as minister by becoming a preacher for the Second Church of York. Moody became an esteemed man of the cloth, presiding over weddings, funerals and other various social events. His sermons were powerful and daunting. But that would soon change as Moody began to shy away from his duties. Some say it was due to the fact that his heart was not into preaching, and he performed such a duty only out of the respect of his father's wishes. Soon Reverend Moody became melancholy to the point where he hid his face from the public by wearing a black veil. Another explanation submitted by historians was that he suffered a severe mental and physical breakdown after his beloved wife and infant daughter died during childbirth.

Either way, Moody began to preach his sermons under the cloak of a black silk veil. This caused much concern with the parishioners, who began to question his mental capacity. Still, his wit was sharp and his sermons fiery. Because of this, many believed the veil was a guise to cover up some physical infliction he may have suffered. Whenever there was a public occasion, the reverend would be present, covered by the macabre veil, sitting with his face toward a wall. His strange behavior, coupled with the black veil, began to take its toll on his profession. His parishioners, though loyal and caring, soon desired other clergy for their occasions.

Moody became a recluse, save for his Sunday sermons and midnight strolls through the burial yard or along the shoreline. More and more, he seemed to shun his own congregation and, at one point, discontinued preaching. This would be short-lived, as he

The veiled minister of York, Maine. *Illustration by Magin Wood.*

soon returned to his chosen profession with full vigor, but the story is not without some legend and, of course, New England–style "yarnin'."

Moody died in 1753. As one legend recounts, it was not until he lay on his deathbed that the reason he bore the strange cover was divulged. Before he died, he called upon a fellow clergyman for final confession. Reverend Moody confessed to him that when he was a young boy, he accidentally killed his best friend while hunting. Fearing the wrath of his father, and more so the possible hatred of his friend's parents, who he revered so, he masked the deed to look like an Indian attack. He used his oratory prowess to convince the village of his concocted story. He was absolved from his act in the eyes of the village, but his soul never healed. After that day, the spirit of his best friend always stood before him, demanding the truth be told.

In remorse for his sins, the reverend later decided he was unfit to look his fellow parsonage in the face and so draped the black silk veil over his head so the pious should never have to look upon the face of sin and guilt. Reverend Moody was buried with the handkerchief over his face as requested, even though he had lifted the veil that had so long covered his soul by final confession.

There is one more fact that can be attested. When Moody was twenty years old, he began to keep a diary written in code and Latin spanning the years 1720 to 1724. The diary was later deciphered, and stories of Indian conflicts, pirates and his many voyages by boat to such places as Marblehead, Isles of Shoals and Gloucester came to life in front of the reader. For example, "1724—They say that Pirates are on the Coast. Gloucester vessels have had a very hard time since they sailed."

According to the deciphered notes, there were hints toward the eccentricity his father exhibited, but readers noted that Joseph Moody followed in his father's footsteps in more ways than one. There is a period of time when Joseph Moody became bitterly disappointed in not securing the hand of his cousin Mary Hirst in marriage. This, some believe, was the point when he became melancholy. Over time, the melancholy turned into a most peculiar behavior, which increased with age.

One can glean much of the circumstance that led to the minister's wearing of the satin covering by perusing the pages of his one-half-inch-by-three-and-one-half-inch journal. In the translating of his writing, many "curious things and eccentric things" were found testifying to the "diseased state of his mind yet mingled with the deepest devotion."

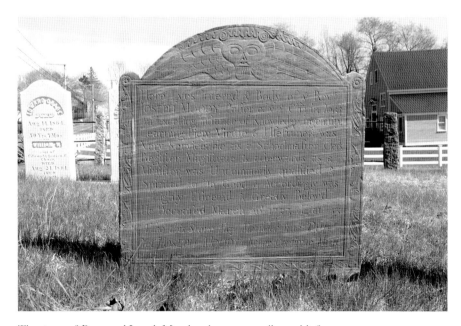

The stone of Reverend Joseph Moody, who wore a veil over his face.

Such a statement alludes to the fact that the reverend had been suffering from some sort of mental illness since his youth or at least after graduating from Harvard. Extracts from the translated work show Moody was infatuated with death and recording the deaths of people around the region. A few extracts from 1720 give example of this:

> *Mr. Lucas died 23*
> *Betty Banks 30*
> *1720–1721 2 men accidently killed at Portsmouth*
> *Capt. Pickerin died 10th April at night*

Although many journals faithfully record deaths of villagers or relatives, the reverend seemed to stretch out and record those he had no society with. In any case, he was precise in writing down what he considered to be pertinent to his world.

Whatever you choose to be your favorite version as to why he wore his veil, it is well known that Joseph "Handkerchief" Moody was liked and admired, according to the epitaph on his stone. Reverend Timothy Alden published his epitaph in 1814, which in full reads:

> *Here lies interred the body of the Reverend Joseph Moody pastor of the Second Church in York, an excelling instance of knowledge, ingenuity, learning, piety, virtue and usefulness, was very serviceable as a schoolmaster, clerk, register, magistrate and afterwards as a minister was uncommonly qualified and spirited to do good, and accordingly was highly esteemed and greatly lamented.*
>
> *Although this stone may moulder into dust,*
> *Yet Joseph Moody's name continue must*

The reverend is buried in a small lot known as the Second Parish Burying Ground on Route 91 across from the Arthur Bragdon House, where he resided for a period during his life.

# LORD TIMOTHY DEXTER

There exist whole tomes on the next character of New England history that were written when those who knew of the "Lord" Dexter were still living. Subsequent writings pepper his life story with the eccentricities of his being, and with good reason; there were many. Timothy Dexter was one of New England's most colorful characters, far surpassing those we often recite during conversations of the region. If the wealthy are burdened to become eccentric, it would be assured Lord Dexter "outpoped the pope" in that category.

Timothy Dexter was born on January 22, 1747, in Malden, Massachusetts. His father was a leather dresser by trade, and as custom of the times, young Timothy was apprenticed into the family business early. The preparation of sheep, goat and deer skins was a necessary and lucrative business during his time, and the Dexter family, although wholly uneducated, did well for themselves.

Dexter soon struck out on his own, marrying a widow of good circumstance and inheritance. The two were frugal yet industrious—virtues that would play well into their future endeavors. The couple had two children, one boy and one girl. Dexter and his wife worked hard to supply the family larder during the hard times preceding the American Revolution. During this period, the Continental dollar (money used by the colonies) had shrunken in value to an almost worthless measure. John Hancock, governor of Massachusetts, and wealthy merchant Thomas Russell began to buy up all of the worthless paper money they could find. Dexter, wanting to be respected as a peer to his neighbors, did the same, using his wife's inheritance to purchase smaller sums of the currency at a better deal no less.

When Alexander Hamilton's funding system finally went into effect, the paper money, as once promised by the famous head of the treasury, became worth its full value, making Dexter a very wealthy man. Dexter now aspired to be in the upper crust of society and fully believed his wealth was all he needed to hobnob with the influential of the day. The fact that he lacked any education or manners of the more refined society was never considered by him as a factor in distinguishing himself as a peer of the great Hancock or Russell.

Dexter and his family moved from Salem to Newburyport, where he purchased a beautiful mansion. The home was a spacious and grand affair, affording a stunning view of the sea. The grounds were laid out in European-style architecture, and the furniture within was of the same taste. A king could ask for no better, but Dexter was only beginning to decorate his newly acquired palace. He raised minarets on the roof surmounted by gilt balls. He then commissioned a young local ship carver named Joseph Wilson to create life-size images for his gardens. These were then placed on fifteen-foot-high columns, about forty in all, in various places around the yard.

Postcard of Lord Timothy Dexter's home. *From the authors' collection.*

The statues were of famous Indian chiefs, military generals, politicians, lions, eagles and mythical figures. He even went as far as having an effigy of himself standing tallest and most conspicuous, with the phrase underneath "I am the first in the east, the first in the west, and the greatest philosopher of the western world." The Roman arch directly in front of the door was reserved for George Washington. To his left was Thomas Jefferson, and to his right stood John Adams. Whenever Dexter passed the statue of Napoleon Bonaparte, he would courteously tip his hat to the wooden gentleman. Dexter also bought a country seat in Chester, New Hampshire, where he proclaimed himself "Lord of Chester."

The fickle Dexter was known to change the names of the statues on a whim. A Bonaparte today could be a Hamilton tomorrow, regardless of the lack of likeness in the figure. At one point, he threatened a painter at musket point to paint "Constitution" on the wooden likeness of what was clearly holding the Declaration of Independence.

Being a lord, Dexter was obligated to have his own coat of arms. He searched a few books and found the one he would call his own. He then purchased a beautiful coach and had matching horses ordered to draw it. After a while, he changed the color of his coach and therefore had to change the color of his horses. So was the mindset of Lord Timothy Dexter.

The rest of the upper class in town were merely amused by his eccentricities and would often take advantage of his simple-mindedness by making up business ventures that may be profitable to him. One man suggested he sell warming pans to people in the East Indies. He managed to convince "Lord Timothy" it gets very chilly down in those parts. Dexter promptly bought and prepared a large shipment to be brought to the East Indies. The ship's captain, upon seeing the ridiculous cargo, and being industrious himself, removed the lids and sold them as skimmers and the pans as ladles for the massive molasses trade. The idea worked beyond measure, and Dexter, much to the embarrassment of his jokers, made a hefty profit.

One time, he was told that there was a shortage of mittens in the East Indies and it would make someone a lot of money to supply the people with such a commodity. Dexter, uneducated about the climate of that region, sent a shipment of mittens forth. The would-be laughter was silenced by the fact that a ship headed for the Baltic region saw the shipment and purchased the whole lot at another great profit for Dexter.

Some call it dumb luck, but whatever it was, Timothy Dexter had it. Another local, knowing of Dexter's feeble intelligence, advised him to invest in whalebone. Lord Dexter, taking the man's advice to heart, purchased as much whalebone as could be had. At first the man and his companions chuckled over his folly, but their chuckles turned to astonishment when the manufacture of women's broad skirts, the latest fashion of the day, required whalebone for the corsets. The bone, being in high demand, sold for quite a profit, and once again, Dexter was there to reap it.

Upon the death of Louis XVI of France, Lord Dexter paid the sexton to ring the church bell in his honor, for he considered himself nobility, and therefore, it was only proper to recognize the passing of one of his "peers." When the French Revolution took place, he sent an invite for the royal family to seek temporary refuge at his home. In pure confidence they would take up his offer, he ordered a large stock of provisions to feed his expected guests for some time to come. They never came, but provisions became scarce, and Dexter was able to unload his surplus, once more, at a tidy profit.

Wishing to be more like his contemporaries Hancock and Russell, Dexter furnished his home with the finest furniture and works from France. In many cases, the furnishings and paintings were more on the unsightly side, and some of the paintings were reported to be forgeries sold to him by uncouth individuals aware of his state of mind. Still, Dexter showed them off with the reverence of a celestial. Being aware of the fine libraries other great men possessed, Dexter also had his furnished with many books, some being fine works while others were completely worthless. Dexter, possessing low reading skill, did not care. It was a library and full of tomes. It can be assured that he probably never read a single volume.

Being idle and rich takes its toll on one, and soon Lord Dexter found himself imbibing in much strong drink. He would take afternoon strolls through the streets of Newburyport dressed in a long coat, large cocked hat and walking cane accompanied by his strange-looking hairless dog. The children in their jest would salute him and call out, "Here comes Lord Timothy Dexter." This amused and satisfied him so much that he would give them money for their salutations.

Many people would stop to stare at his eccentric abode, which also pleased him. His gardens of fine fruits and vegetables were among the finest in the town. Dexter began to fear that the "common folk" of the town were pillaging his bounty. He hired a sentry to keep watch in the night so no one would sneak in and steal his fruits. After a while, Dexter became suspicious that the watchman may be sleeping on the job or in league with any would-be poachers and made this clear to the townsfolk. The next night, two shots from a musket rang out, waking the occupants of the house. When they encountered the sentry, he was in agony over his deed and laid full blame on Dexter, who was delighted by the situation. A tree limb was broken, and there were traces of blood found along with footprints in the sand heading out to the street.

Lord Dexter was so excited that his guard had done his job that he rewarded him with fifty pounds of coffee from a shipment that had just been delivered. He asked his wife to weigh up the exact measure, and when presented to the man, the sack appeared to be much too small for the specified weight. He ordered it weighed in front of him and made clear that the shortage would come from his wife's share fivefold. The watchman was awarded the extra amount, which was now impossible to carry alone. A cart was brought in to transport the supply of coffee back to the sentry's home.

Lord Dexter's son Samuel Lord Dexter soon came of the age where he may be weaned in the family business. Unfortunately, Samuel was known to be "imbecile" in intellect. Nonetheless, Lord Dexter sent him with a cargo to England, where he lost the entire shipment at the gambling table.

One day, in one of his drunken stupors, Dexter ordered his son to shoot a man whom he suspected was trying to gain access to his cherry trees. The son outright refused, so Dexter took his pistol and fired at the passerby. Luckily, he was too drunk to aim straight, and the ball hit the fence. The man complained to the magistrates, and Dexter was sentenced to several months in jail. When the time came, he made a deal with the sheriff that he could ride to the jailhouse in his coach with the sheriff following behind. All the way to the clink, Lord Dexter joked and remarked that no one had ever ridden to jail in such class and splendor.

Dexter desired to be buried in a vault on his property and had an elaborate chamber constructed in the gardens as his eternal home. Hearing that the likes of Hancock and Russell would have beautiful coffins, he ordered a special coffin made of mahogany with silver handles. He then put the coffin in the house as an exhibit for those who would visit.

In one of his drunken states, he came up with the notion that he would like to test his fame and popularity by holding a mock funeral. Invitations and cards were sent out, and the people came. No minister in his right mind would perform for such folly, so the job was given to one of the townsfolk. After the ceremony, the coffin was laid in the vault, and all were invited into the grand room for food and drink. The finest meal and liquor was liberally served. One guest pointed out that he swore he saw the late Lord Dexter in an upstairs window looking out over the guests. The revelry was suddenly interrupted by screams. The throng rushed into the next room, where Lord Dexter, much alive, was caning his wife. During the ceremony, he noticed she was not shedding enough tears.

Lord Dexter heard many great men had poet laureates to pen their adventures for others to read. He was not to be overlooked in this category. He hired a poet by the name of Jonathan Plummer to write verses of his exploits, wealth and greatness.

One of the most lasting exploits comes in the writing of his book *A Pickle for the Knowing Ones*. Dexter had heard that many rich and famous people wrote books that they gave away as gifts. Lord Dexter was compelled to do the same. He had thousands of copies made and gave them freely, thus increasing his notoriety. The book is still in print but is as difficult to digest as it was when first penned. By all standards, it was a hodgepodge of some sensible, mostly non-sensible gibberish opinions of the author. The grammar is based on his lack of education and in some cases almost impossible to decipher. All sentences are jumbled together with no punctuation, making it difficult to read or understand. When this was commented on, Dexter made a note for the printer for the second edition: "Mister printer the Nowing Ones complane of my book the first edition had no stops I put anuf here and thay may peper and solt it as they plese." The last page of the book contained line after line of assorted punctuation marks!

# A Pickle for the Knowing Ones

## Plain Truth in a Homespun Dress

# Lord Timothy Dexter

*Above*: Lord Timothy Dexter's now famous book, hailed as one of the most horrible works ever published.

*Right*: His fame even created the need for a spoon in his name.

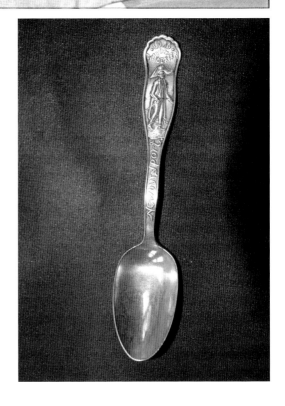

Lord Timothy Dexter passed on October 23, 1806. During his time in jail, sobriety had made him think of his actions, and during his last days, he was aware that such events made him the joke of the town. In his attempt to atone for his dealings, he made a will dispersing his wealth to those he felt would benefit from it.

Upon his death, the town decided not to have him buried in the grand vault he had erected in his garden. The board of health was adamant in this decision, deciding that the grave of such a person would cause much disruption in the town. Instead, Dexter was buried in the Hill Cemetery in Newburyport with a simple stone marking his grave.

In a bit of irony, if Dexter was searching for fame, he may have been ridiculed for his doings in life, but he has certainly reached an immortal status in death for the amusing life he led. In fact, he has become one of New England's and certainly Newburyport's most colorful characters.

# Frozen Vermonters

My mother's side of our family originated from Canada before migrating across the border and settling in Swanton, Vermont. This next tale is an old family recollection that was written many years ago, and I am proud to relate the tale that Allen Morse made famous. The story appeared in the *Rutland Herald* and *Boston Globe* in 1939. *Yankee* magazine later printed the story. Many other periodicals and books would follow. The *Old Farmer's Almanac* brought eventual worldwide exposure to the accounts "witnessed" by Mr. Morse in 1887. Presented below is the story that has been told and retold for more than a century.

### "A Strange Tale," by Allen Morse

I am an old man now, and have seen some strange sights in the course of a roving life in foreign lands as well as in this country, but none so strange as one I found recorded in an old diary, kept by my Uncle William, that came into my possession a few years ago, at his decease. The events described took place in a mountain town some twenty miles from Montpelier, the Capital of Vermont. I have been to the place on the mountain, and seen the old log-house where the events I found recorded in the diary took place, and seen and talked with an old man who vouched for the truth of the story, and that his father was one of the parties operated on. The account runs in this wise:

"January 7.—I went on the mountain today, and witnessed what to me was a horrible sight. It seems that the dwellers there, who are unable, either from age or other reasons, to contribute to the support of their families, are disposed of in the winter months in a manner that will shock the one who reads this diary, unless that person lives in that vicinity. I will describe what I saw. Six persons, four men and two women, one of the men a cripple about 30 years old, the other five past the age of usefulness, lay on the earthy floor of the cabin drugged into insensibility, while members of their families were gathered about them in apparent indifference. In a short time the unconscious bodies were inspected by one man who said, 'They are ready.' They were then stripped of all their clothing, except a single garment. Then the bodies were carried outside, and laid on logs exposed to the bitter cold mountain air, the operation having been delayed several days for suitable weather.

"It was night when the bodies were carried out, and the full moon, occasionally obscured by flying clouds, shone on their upturned ghastly faces, and a horrible fascination kept me by the bodies as long as I could endure the severe cold. Soon the noses, ears and fingers began to turn white, then the limbs and face assumed a tallowy look. I could stand the cold no longer, and went inside, where I found the friends in cheerful conversation.

"In about an hour I went out and looked at the bodies: they were fast freezing. Again I went inside, where the men were smoking their clay pipes, but silence had fallen on them; perhaps they were thinking of the time when their turn would come to be cared for in the same way. One by one they at last lay down on the floor, and went to sleep. It seemed a horrible nightmare to me, and I could not think of sleep. I could not shut out the sight of those freezing bodies outside, neither could I bear to be in darkness, but I piled on the wood in the cavernous fireplace, and, seated on a shingle block, passed the dreary night, terror-stricken by the horrible sights I had witnessed.

"January 8.—Day came at length, but did not dissipate the terror that filled me. The frozen bodies became visible, white as the snow that lay in huge drifts about them. The women gathered about the fire, and soon commenced preparing breakfast. The men awoke, and, conversation again commencing, affairs assumed a more cheerful aspect. After breakfast the men lighted their pipes, and some of them took a yoke of oxen and went off toward the forest, while others proceeded to nail together boards, making a box about ten feet long and half as high and wide. When this was completed they placed about two feet of straw in the bottom; then they laid three of the frozen bodies on the straw. Then the faces and upper part of the bodies were covered with a cloth, then more straw was put in the box, and the other three bodies placed on top and covered the same as the first ones, with cloth and straw. Boards were then firmly nailed on the top, to protect the bodies from being injured by carnivorous animals that make their home on these mountains.

"By this time the men who went off with the ox-team returned with a huge load of spruce and hemlock boughs, which they unloaded at the foot of a steep ledge, came to the house and loaded the box containing the bodies on the sled, and drew it to the foot of the ledge, near the load of boughs. These were soon piled on and around the box, and it was left to be covered up with snow, which I was told would lie in drifts twenty feet deep over this rude tomb. 'We shall want our men to plant our corn next spring,' said a youngish looking woman, the wife of one of the frozen men, 'and if you want to see them resuscitated, you come here about the 10th of next May.'

"With this agreement, I left the mountaineers, both the living and the frozen, to their fate and I returned to my home in Boston where it was weeks before I was fairly myself, as my thoughts would return to that mountain with its awful sepulcher." Turning the leaves of the diary to the date of May 10, the following entry was found:

"May 10—I arrived here at 10 am, after riding about four hours over muddy, unsettled roads. The weather is warm and pleasant, most of the snow is gone, except here and there drifts in the fence corners and hollows, but nature is not yet dressed in green. I found the same parties here that I left last January, ready to disinter the bodies of their friends. I had no expectation of finding any life there, but a feeling that I could not resist impelled me to come and see. We repaired at once to the well remembered spot, at the ledge. The snow had melted from the top of the brush, but still lay deep around the bottom of the pile. The men commenced work at once, some shoveling away the snow, and others tearing away the brush. Soon the box was visible. The cover was taken off, the layers of straw removed, and the bodies, frozen and apparently lifeless, lifted out and laid on the snow.

"Large troughs made out of hemlock logs were placed nearby, filled with tepid water, into which the bodies were separately placed, with the head slightly raised. Boiling water was then poured into the trough from kettles hung on poles over fires near by, until the water in the trough was as hot as I could hold my hand in. Hemlock boughs had been put in the boiling water in such quantities that they had given the water the color of wine. After lying in this bath about an hour, color began to return to the bodies, when all hands began rubbing and chafing them. This continued about another hour, when a slight twitching of the muscles of the face and limbs, followed by audible gasps, showed that life was not quenched, and that vitality was returning. Spirits were then given in small quantities, and allowed to trickle down their throats. Soon they could swallow, and more was given them, when their eyes opened, and they began to talk, and finally sat up in their bath-tubs. They were then taken out and assisted to the house, where after a hearty dinner they seemed as well as ever, and in nowise injured, but rather refreshed, by their long sleep of four months."

So, THERE YOU HAVE it. Believable? To many, yes. Science has proven that we can freeze animate objects and later on restore them after thawing. Were these Vermonters ahead of their time or was Mr. Morse a grand teller of tales? Allen Morse was a dairy farmer from Calais. He was born in 1835 and died in 1917. He was known to be the king of "yarnin'." When the old folks got together to tell stories, the next would have to top the previous. It was entertaining in those days to while away the hours by a country store wood stove and spin fantastic "true" accounts they had witnessed in their lives. How much was actually true? That is the real mysterious part of this tale.

# THE MELON HEADS OF CONNECTICUT

Almost all Connecticut residents have heard of the legendary Melon Heads. Who they are or where they came from is a mystery yet to be solved—that is, of course, maintaining they exist in the first place. Many consider the band of large-pated folk to be an urban legend, while others swear they have encountered these odd people wandering the back roads in the dead of night.

The Melon Heads are said to be a group of deformed mutant inbreeds living in obscurity around Connecticut, especially New Haven and Fairfield Counties. They have large bulbous heads and bulging eyes. They do not speak to anyone and stare straight ahead when encountered. There are several places they have been spotted, all being rarely traveled roads in rural areas. The versions of their origin seem to vary quite considerably. One states that a family shunned by society began inbreeding and has never stopped. Another contributes the size of their heads to encephalitis (swelling of the brain). One person may have contracted this illness many years ago and shied from society to hide his hideous appearance, thus creating the origin of the legend. Another account states they were escapees from a Fairfield County mental hospital that burned down in 1960. After the fire, about a dozen patients were unaccounted for. Many believe these patients escaped into the woods and began living off the land and breeding. There are also claims that they descended from a family of witches living in solitude. Another plausible answer is that they were a mixture of European and Native American peoples called Melungeon. These people descended from the mixed couples dating back to colonial times. All theories conclude with the fact that they look hideously abnormal due to excessive inbreeding generation after generation.

There are many roads in the state where the Melon Heads are reported to wander, including Downs Road in Hamden, Saw Mill City Road in Shelton and Velvet Road that runs through Trumbull and Monroe at the Easton border, also known as Dracula Drive. Other roads include Edmonds Road in Oxford, Zion Hill Road in Milford, Jeremy Swamp Road in Southbury and Marginal Road in New Haven. The roads around Lake Mohegan and Roosevelt State Forest in Stratford are also reported to be home to the strange creatures.

Melon Heads are reported to be cannibalistic and will devour whoever enters their domain. Whether anyone has ever been eaten by them is a matter of conjecture, but the legends of their existence persist and seem to grow over time. In fact, some have claimed to see them shopping in grocery stores or malls. Neither author of this book has ever witnessed the Melon Heads while traveling through the many back roads of Connecticut, but it can be assured that if these strange people were spied, it would not be an opportune time to stop and take a photo. In any case, if you should be driving one of the numerous rustic dirt roads mentioned above, keep your eyes peeled for the large-headed, bulgy-eyed characters that roam the areas in the dark bowers of the night as one of New England's strange characters.

# Frozen Alive

This strange tale took place and was recorded in 1850. The characters led an everyday life until this moment, and the ending of the account will surely be a true-to-the-word example of New England's grotesque and fantastic.

Richard Ingraham and his fiancée, Lydia Dyer, held up safely on their schooner accompanied by a seaman named Roger Elliott. It was December 22, and a storm suddenly struck the Maine coast. Bitter cold, violent winds and blizzard conditions blanketed the area around Rockland, where the waves could be heard booming mercilessly upon all in their path. The weather was so frigid that the waves turned to ice upon impact with the land.

The three held fast and safe in the little schooner cabin until around midnight, when they heard cables snap, and the ship began to race out toward the sea. The anchor cables had snapped, and there was no stopping the vessel as it crashed on the ledges near Owl's Head. In an instant, the three grabbed all the blankets they could and rushed to the deck, but the driving blizzard and howling winds made it impossible for them to see anything, much less signal for help.

In a last-ditch effort to save their lives in the deadly storm, they huddled on the floor of the now exposed cabin and covered their bodies with blankets. The ice formed quickly over them, but Elliott, having a knife, was able to cut a hole for them to breathe continually. They were confident the ice would insulate them and keep them alive until help arrived.

The storm soon let up enough that Elliott, who had positioned himself on top of the couple, could cut through the layer of ice and scale the ledges for help. He made his way up the ledge, exhausted, frostbitten and bloody, yet undaunted. Soon he was spotted and rescued, at which point he collapsed, but not before letting the rescuer know there were two more on the wreck.

The rescue party arrived at the wrecked schooner, where they saw the couple's frozen bodies, motionless and covered in a tomb of ice. The tide began to rise, and the rescue party knew they had but moments to remove the couple from the ship. They carefully removed the giant block of ice that entombed the couple and transported it to a nearby home. There, they began to thaw the two out. As they chipped and peeled the ice from the lovers' bodies, they could only fear the worst.

Once the bodies were removed from the ice block, rescuers placed the two in a tub, poured cold water over them and gradually increased the water's warmth. The rescuers softly massaged the lifeless bodies of the two to resuscitate them. All efforts seemed futile for a few hours, but then the most improbable happened—Dyer awoke from her frozen slumber. An hour later, Ingraham's body turned and moved with life. "What is all this?" he asked.

He looked over and saw his fiancée, who smiled back at him. They were both alive. Within months, they had made a full recovery. They were married in June 1851 and went on to lead a normal and prosperous life together. Elliott, the man responsible for their safe return, never fully recovered from his injuries but still lived to tell his accounts of the tale.

# THE GREEN PEOPLE OF COVENTRY

No, they were not aliens from outer space—at least that anyone was aware of. This tale has been told and retold by the people of Coventry, Rhode Island, for many years.

It seems that from 1950 to the 1970s, there lived a family in Coventry known as "the green people." They made their abode in a run-down shack deep in the woods with rusty old cars rambling among other piles of garbage and whatnot strewn about the yard. Just the scenery alone was enough to attract the locals' attention, but what really had the town talking was their hair and skin color. It was a pale green.

They mostly kept to themselves, going into town for essentials or bringing the children to school. They were not malicious or rude, yet they never spoke much to anyone outside their family. A plausible, scientific explanation why they were such a color may have been the high copper content in the water of their well.

No one knew much about the green people, as the family maintained an elusive lifestyle. Time rolled on, and they just seemed to vanish from the earth. The decrepit home was eventually demolished and the garbage cleared away. Any other information on the green people disappeared with them. Who knows—maybe they were aliens or creatures from another planet or at least another realm in this world.

# PHINEAS GAGE

On September 13, 1848, an event stunned the medical field when the improbable happened in Cavendish, Vermont. Twenty-five-year-old Phineas Gage, a blasting foreman for the Rutland and Burlington Railroad, was using his three-foot tamping iron to set explosive charges in a rock ledge when it prematurely exploded, sending the iron through his skull. Setting the blast entailed boring a hole in the rock and adding blasting powder and a fuse. Sand was used to fill in the rest of the hole before tamping down the whole mixture with the rod.

Around 4:30 p.m., Gage was distracted while tamping one of the holes. He turned his head to speak to a co-worker, and at the same time, the rod accidentally struck the rock, igniting the powder. The one-and-a-quarter-inch-diameter, three-foot-seven-inch custom-made rod blew straight through Gage's upper jaw, passed behind his left eye and through the left side of his brain before exiting his skull. The rod landed eighty feet away, taking part of his brain with it. Gage, still conscious, was assisted as he walked partway back to town. Physician Edward Williams was brought to the scene, where Gage simply said, "Doctor, here is business enough for you."

Dr. John Harlow took charge of the case from there. With Williams's help, Harlow removed bone fragments and an ounce of protruding brain while cleaning the wound, replacing some of the bone and dressing it. Harlow also attended to the burns Gage suffered on his hands and arms from the blast.

Gage recovered, but slowly and with ups and downs regarding mental capacity. Further surgery was needed, and within a month, Gage was walking about and talking. Ten weeks later, he returned to his parents' home in Lebanon, New Hampshire.

News spread quickly of the man who had a three-foot iron rod blast through his skull, and he soon became an attraction. People packed into theaters to see the man, with rod in hand, tell his story. He became somewhat of a celebrity, but friends and family knew something was different. He was now prone to fits of anger and began having epileptic seizures. When it passed through his skull, the rod had taken his frontal lobe and sight in his left eye.

A plaque commemorating the Phineas Gage incident in Cavendish, Vermont. *Courtesy of Vickie and Bob Hughes.*

Gage later moved west, where he found work as a stagecoach driver, but illness began to take its toll on the once strong and industrious man. By February 1860, Phineas Gage was experiencing regular epileptic seizures. His mother and sister moved west to care for him, but on May 21, 1860, thirty-six-year-old Gage died during one of his seizures and was buried in San Francisco's Lone Mountain Cemetery. Gage had survived the accident for twelve years.

In 1866, his body was disinterred, and his skull and iron tamping bar were given to Dr. Harlow, the man who had cared for him after the accident. Dr. Harlow later gave the artifacts to Harvard Medical School's Warren Anatomical Museum, where they have been on display since. In 1940, Gage's headless remains were relocated to Cypress Lawn Cemetery when the city passed a law requiring the dead to be buried outside city limits. There is a monument and walking tour in Cavendish telling the tale of the incident. To this day, the story of Phineas Gage is an enigma to science, but in New England, as we have seen repeatedly, truth is often stranger than fiction.

# HELEN DOW PECK'S AMAZING WILL

When the Ouija board hit the market in 1891, it became an immediate success. Four investors saw it as not necessarily a doorway into the unknown as much as a doorway into the American people's wallets. By the turn of the twentieth century, countless boards were in use in American homes.

People from all walks of life used the board to connect with the deceased or add some merriment in times of strife. World Wars I and II, the 1918 flu pandemic and the Great Depression saw millions turning to the board in hopes of contacting lost ones or gaining insight on the future. One woman, Helen Dow Peck of Danbury, Connecticut, communicated with her board's spirit and would later vow to take very good care of her formless friend.

Upon Peck's death in 1955 at the age of eighty-three, she left a will with a most curious request. The will clearly stated that widow Peck's two servants were to receive $1,000 each for their services, and a man named John Gale Forbes was to receive $178,000, the rest of her estate. This was indeed a bizarre situation considering Mr. Forbes did not exist—at least in the flesh.

Mrs. Peck related to family and friends that the name had appeared to her and her husband, Frank, during a 1919 Ouija board session. For the next thirty-four years, Peck would search in vain for John Gale Forbes's physical being, without success. Forbes, according to Mrs. Peck, did appear

Millions of Ouija boards have been sold since its inception in 1891 by the Kennard Toy Company. *Photo by Arlene Nicholson from the authors' collection.*

to her once during a session. Mrs. Peck had told friends that Forbes "had resolved out of space" about 1940 while using the board, the same one that she had owned since 1919. He also provided her with advice. Mrs. Peck was genuinely convinced Forbes not only existed but was living in a mental institution somewhere using mental telepathy to reach out to her. Although she never located his whereabouts, in her will, Peck requested that if Forbes or his heirs could not be found, a trust was to be established with her money as a memorial fund for the study of telepathy among the insane.

Nine nieces and nephews contested the will, claiming their aunt lacked testamentary capacity and the will was void because of its uncertainty. The City National Bank of Danbury disagreed, stating that Forbes may have been a real person. A private investigator, working on the bank's assertion, never found John Gale Forbes.

After three years of strange testimony and a lot of searching for Mr. Forbes or any possible relatives, the state supreme court decided to reject the will. In 1958, widow Peck's heirs received the remainder of her estate.

What would a spirit have done with the money anyway? Perhaps store it in the cloud?

# WHERE DID EPHRIAM GRAY GO?

The secret of immortality. Many people have attempted to concoct a potion, spell or some other way to live throughout eternity unscathed by the ravages of time. Impossible, you say? Well, one man may have cheated the reaper and, to this day, lives among the masses unchanged by the passing of the years. That man was, or perhaps still is, Ephriam Gray.

Ephriam lived as a recluse in a large house in the center of Malden, Massachusetts, during the early to mid-1800s with his male servant. The hired hand took care of all outside business and chores while Ephriam toiled through the late hours in a makeshift laboratory in his apartment. The neighbors frequently inquired as to the nature of Gray's work and the foul odors that often emanated from his chambers' windows. The servant slyly dodged their queries with a joke or passing comment of no real meaning.

For years, the goings-on inside those walls remained a mystery until one morning in 1850, when Gray's manservant showed up at the police station claiming his employer had passed during the night. He explained that Ephriam had, for many years, experimented in attempts to create an elixir that would grant him immortality. Although he had tested his attempts countless times, he expired before he could perfect the formula.

The servant gave explicit instructions for Gray's body to be taken and buried immediately, as there was no need for embalming or autopsy. According to the hired hand, Gray's body was more than preserved due to his experiments' constant imbibing. The explicit instructions were carried out to the letter, and Gray's body was quickly committed to a small crypt in the center of the town cemetery. The servant lived in the home for several more years before he, too, passed away. The legends and tales of Ephriam's experiments eventually reached the ears of a group of Harvard medical students who became tempted to see if the stories were real and his body was still preserved.

One dark evening in 1870, the throng crept out into the cemetery to the crypt where Ephriam lay in repose. Upon entering the burial chamber, they pried the lid off the coffin and stammered back in awe. The body of Ephriam Gray had not decayed even the slightest in the twenty years it lay in the casket. The students quickly resealed the coffin, returned to Cambridge and swore among themselves never to tell anyone of their discovery, for it was assured they would be expelled from medical school or, even worse, be charged with the crime of grave robbing.

In 1900, the advent of a new invention, the automobile, called for wider and better-paved roads, making it necessary to relocate the cemetery. The crews began moving the bodies and stones to a new location without any occurrences until they came to Ephriam Gray's casket. When they hoisted the coffin, they found it to be unusually light. Upon opening the box, the bewildered grave diggers found it to be void of a tenant. Gray's body had vanished. It was not long before word got out around the region, causing the former medical students, now in their middle age, to come forth and swear they never touched the body. All asserted to have taken extreme care in resealing the coffin and carefully placing it back in its original resting place, with Gray's body inside.

The whereabouts of Ephriam Gray's body have never been determined. Could he have discovered the secret to immortality? Perhaps he walks to this day among the mortal souls as they meander through their aging life, moving on before anyone begins to wonder why they turn old and gray, yet Gray stays young and vibrant.

# Vagabonds and Wanderers

## The Darn Man

The "Darn Man" or "Old Darn Coat" continues our extraordinary trip through New England's strange inhabitants. If it was not for historian Ellen Larned, the following character's chronicles might have disappeared into obscurity. Surely that would not be such a place for one of his distinction in our region's history. Larned appealed to several publications for information regarding the Darn Man who once roamed the highways and byways of eastern Connecticut, southern Massachusetts and western Rhode Island. Her 1906 request was met with surprising results. There were many people still alive who remembered this charismatic wanderer of the New England countryside. It is the remembrances of those people that may best tell the story of the mysterious rambling pedestrian you shall now become more acquainted with.

No one knew for sure when he appeared on the New England landscape. The Darn Man emerged seemingly out of nowhere and continued his circuit with a ceaseless and precise regimen for fifty years, roaming from town to town in southeast New England.

Larned's request included a short description of the wandering soul:

> *Many years ago, a weird figure was often seen hurrying along the roads and byways of Windham County, spectral and gaunt with bent form and long white hair, heedless of passerby or curious query, pausing at some*

*accustomed farmhouse for needle and thread to darn his much worn suit and for food and a night's lodging.*

Among the many replies Larned received, a certain George Griggs, who lived in Woodstock with his aunt Mrs. Ebenezer Skinner around 1863, recounted his memories of the spring-heeled wanderer. The Skinner home was among the many places the Darn Man chose as a regular stop along his route. In February of that year, young man Griggs set out to the barn to complete the night's chores. A winter storm covered the ground with several inches of snow, making his task all the more difficult. Undaunted, he continued his routine until he saw something in the snow. Griggs wrote this account in 1906:

> *I chanced to notice a bundle on the side of the snow path, and soon recognized it as the prostrate form of our monthly visitor. I aroused him and gently aided him to the house where my aunt fed and warmed him. He remained with us for three days. My aunt had a good room and bed always reserved for his accommodations.*

Another person who replied to the query was W.B. Fox of Norwich. The Darn Man would visit his former home in Hampton, Connecticut, quite often. He would never beg for anything but request only needles and thread to darn his suit, which, by Fox's recollection, was already a mass of multicolored thread and yarn from previous repairs. When he wanted to eat, he would walk into the kitchen and seat himself at the table of some familiar house. And according to all who knew him, he was never denied or turned away from a repast.

One time, the Darn Man showed up at the home of a stranger. The man answered the door, knowing full well who the wanderer was. In turn, the Darn Man implored the homeowner that he may sleep there for the night. The owner politely asked him, "Why don't you go home? Where is your home anyway?" He replied, "Anywhere the night overtakes me, if they will please let me stay." The man welcomed him into his home and never questioned his occasional guest again.

A Windham County woman remembered her encounters with the Darn Man and recounted them in writing for a literary society in 1889:

> *This strange name belonged to a tall white figure, whose rapid, gliding step and ghostly appearance made one question whether he was really of*

*this world and not some visitor from the realms of shadow. I remember him as an old man, his form slightly bowed, his long white hair falling down his neck, his earnest look forward, never seeming to notice anyone as he passed along….He stopped at certain places and with the elegance of a Chesterfield, asked for some slight refreshment, or for a cup of tea. None had higher appreciation of the merits of the fragrant beverage. With a canister of the best tea given him, he would make a cup that a celestial would enjoy.*

He was very selective of the homes he chose for his sojourns, desiring only those honored to receive his company. Thomas Bennett of Canterbury recalled the Old Darn Man making his way into town twice a year, calling for needle and thread with which he would darn the rents in his clothes. Bennett's father was a shoemaker. Bennett reminisced how the Old Darn Man would enter his father's shop, take the worn heels off his shoes and replace them himself. Bennett also recollected that the Darn Man was an avid tea drinker, as attested by all who kept society with him in their homes.

Mr. A.D. Ayer recounted much about the Darn Man, including his fondness for tea. He often prepared the beverage himself, making it exceptionally strong, and would drink several cups, sampling each one until it suited his taste. Ayer recollected the legend attributing to his unusual lifestyle. This story has taken on some alterations over the centuries, but the main essence seems that he was to be married, and his bride died suddenly, leaving him waiting at the altar in his wedding suit. It was this suit he wore to her funeral and donned the rest of his wandering days incessantly. It is generally accepted that he took to wandering his circuit after his betrothed's death because of a mental breakdown suffered from that fateful day. Some claim he walked the byways of the region in a never-ending search for his lost bride.

Ayer described what he knew of the Darn Man in *A Modern History of Windham County, Connecticut*, volume 2, by Allen B. Lincoln. From April 1859 to around 1860, the Darn Man appeared regularly at Hampton, also known as Goshen and Clark's Corners. Ayer's mother received bits and pieces of the traveler's life during these visits. Ayer reported:

*He had on that same coat he was wearing when he went to a certain place— he would not say whether it was a church or a house—to be married. The bride never came; he never knew what became of her. He then said he would never wear any other coat until he found her. So as time went on, when a hole or tear came, he darned it with many colored threads, strings and yarns; hence his name, old "Darn Coat." He usually wore a tall or stovepipe hat, in which he carried his glasses, kerchief, and a nice snuffbox with gold inlaid in the cover, which a woman had given him years before I knew him, and in the snuffbox was the bean which all snuff users had in their boxes. He was a man who was well posted in current events and past history. He was a great reader.* My father had a regular reading list, the Hartford Weekly Times, New York Ledger *(Bonner's)*, Harper's Illustrated Weekly, *occasionally, the* Boston True Flag, Saturday Evening Post *(Philadelphia), and mother had* Ladies' Magazine. *The "Darn Man" asked, soon after he began to come to our house, if he could not work a little and stay two or three days, so that he could read more. He seemed to be much interested in mother's magazine. He would call her attention to a woman in a new style of dress, and then would sit down and gaze at it for a long time. Mother would ask him if it carried him back to the young woman he expected to marry when he saw those pictures, and he would say, "If I told you, you would know my thoughts, my memories of the past." Never would he give a straight answer.*

The Darn Man was also educated in music. Ayer and others who knew him were occasionally given concerts on the itinerant's violin. Although the Ayer family never found out his real name or place of birth, they suspected he might have been of English origin, as he spoke of the country and people as if he had firsthand knowledge. His visits were regular, arriving once a month from April to January. Where he sojourned in the interim months was a mystery to the family. He was also known to be neat and well groomed. He always cleaned himself and his garb whenever possible. Ayer went on to state:

*At times he carried an umbrella—he must have picked it up—quite a bit of money, for he had some with him. He would talk about the way English people did in order to get on the throne and was especially down on queens, relating their treachery, for example, Mary and her sister, telling how you can trust some women, their word is good, but most of them are only for themselves. He would turn to me and say, "Boy, as you grow up, beware of the girls. Don't spend your money on them. Don't pay out for a nice wedding suit, especially a coat, for you may be left as I was, to wander about with my wedding coat I avowed to wear until I learned what became of the one whom I had adored, who I am not willing to say went back on me; I am charitable enough to think she was spirited away or lost her mind and perhaps was killed."*

The Ayer family had earned his trust more than others, for he once told the family that his name was Thompson from New Bedford, and he had two brothers who were farmers. After the family left Hampton and moved to Scotland, Connecticut, they saw the Darn Man a few more times. When asked why he did not change his route to pay them a visit in their new home, he replied, "No, I have my mind made up to keep on going over the same route, in the same towns, and I expect to die some time in some of the places I have been for years."

When asked if he would, in confidence, reveal the names of some relatives who may be contacted in the event of his passing or any money he had to go to someone as an inheritance, he merely stated, "If you knew what I know about myself, you would know what I know."

Allen Jewett, also of Hampton, recalled how the Darn Man often stayed at his home. He described him as tall and thin, with small features, slender hands and blue eyes. He wore a swallowtail coat, tight-fitting pants, vest and stovepipe hat. He drank lots of tea and ate little. He told Mr. Jewett's mother his name was George Johnson, and he had two sisters living in Rhode Island.

Pertaining to his penchant for tea, the Darn Man was quite an aficionado. He would always ask for a cup of tea at his stops; in fact, he carried a special cloth to wrap tea leaves. He often would ask the lady of the house if he could prepare the beverage so it would be to his liking. Whenever he stayed the night, he would join the family for breakfast. As soon as he had finished, he would stand, remove his hat, bow his head and recite a grateful thanks and appreciation for their hospitality in a most gentlemanly manner. He would then continue his way to the next stop, wherever that may be. As for the cause of his wanderings, stories included his bride dying at sea upon returning with her wedding dress and leaving him standing at the altar. Another report is that he was to be married in New London, but his betrothed died of a sudden sickness. According to the man, she never showed up for the wedding and was never heard from again, which is why he took to his itinerant manner of living, ceaselessly marching the same circuit, some claim, searching for his bride.

As time wore on, the Darn Man began to lose the spring in his stride. His gait became less enthusiastic; his tall, slender figure hunched over with age; and his youthful look became scarred with sunken, saddened eyes. In late November 1863, he died on the road between Sterling, Connecticut, and

Foster, Rhode Island. Elisha Anderson found him frozen on the side of the road and assisted in carrying the old man to his farmhouse. Unfortunately, the Darn Man did not make it to the home before passing. It is reported that Anderson buried the man in the family lot. It was later reported that the Darn Man's real name was Addison Thompson, but some stated it was Moses Thompson and others insisted he was Frank Howland, a descendant of the *Mayflower* Howlands.

Whoever the Darn Man was may be shrouded in mystery for all time. Attempts to find his final resting place were met with failure. It appears time, progress and the lack of perpetuation regarding his existence have all but obliterated the legacy of the wanderer we may forever know only as the "Darn Man" or "Old Darn Coat."

# Old Coot of Mount Greylock

In 1861, a North Adams farmer named William Saunders, like many of his time, left his home to fight for the Union in the Civil War. Saunders kissed his wife and children goodbye on the promise of a speedy return. During his tenure as a soldier, he wrote faithfully to his wife, Belle, who waited anxiously for her beloved to come home. About a year after enlistment, a letter arrived at her door stating he had been seriously wounded by a cannonball in battle and was not likely to survive his injuries. This would be the last correspondence she would receive in regard to her husband.

Her sorrow was deep, for she feared the worst of his fate, yet she needed to tend to the farm. She hired a young man named Milton Clifford to help with the work while she and the children did what they could. As time passed, she realized that her husband must have perished in the war and eventually married Milton, who, in turn, adopted her children.

The War Between the States ended in 1865, and the soldiers of both sides went back to their respective lives. One of these was a bearded, weathered farmer named William Saunders, who had survived his injuries only to continue fighting for the cause. Saunders made his way back to his home, gaunt, tired and ragged yet eager to reunite with his wife and children, who were but babies when he left.

His joy turned to disbelief when, from afar, he saw his wife in the arms of another man whom his children now called "Daddy." This devastated the poor Saunders, who realized his family had gone on without him during his absence. Instead of encountering them to announce he had come home, he

Old Coot of Mount Greylock. *Courtesy of* Berkshire Eagle.

turned and headed toward Mount Greylock, where he built a crude cabin in the remote portion of Bellows Pipe. There he lived out the rest of his days, occasionally working at local farms for his necessities. The locals called him "Old Coot," as he never gave them a proper name. This moniker he was happy to accept. No one he knew before recognized him due to the injuries he suffered in battle and the aging beyond his years from the rigors of the war. It is said that he even helped at his own farm, sometimes joining his family for meals. Whenever he faced his family, it was with his long, straggly hair covering what was left of his gaunt face. To say he may have gone insane, either from the war or over losing his family, was an understatement. Either way, one cold winter day in January, hunters stumbled upon his shack, where they found Old Coot dead. They were more than frightened when his spirit jumped from his body, bolted out the door and flew up the mountainside. To this day, his "bedraggled spirit" is seen on Mount Greylock, always ascending the peak but never reversing direction.

Bellows Pipe derives its name from the wind that whistles through the pines, making the sound of a large pipe being blown into. Is it the wind, or could it be the wailing of a sad spirit that left for a good cause only to be left behind?

## LEATHER MAN

Of all the strange characters in New England, few have captured the heart and quills like the roving itinerant once known, among other names, as the "Leather Man." There were once tales that he was a man named Jules Bourglay from Lyons, France, but they have long since been put to rest.

Leather Man was first seen in April 1858 in the town of Harwinton. Dressed from head to toe in a heavy leather hat, large overcoat, thick trousers, shoes made from wooden soles with leather tops and a large side bag for carrying his possessions, he roamed the countryside, sleeping in caves and stopping in nearby towns for food. He would partake in the provisions gifted to him by certain townsfolk and move on. He was known to travel in a clockwise 365-mile circuit. Every thirty-four days, he would be back at the same place he was on the previous loop. Townsfolk could set their clocks by his arrival.

Leather Man never spoke many distinguishable syllables of the English language to anyone. His form of communication was mostly gestures and grunts in French, yet he became quite the icon in Connecticut and New York State. His arrival into town was so prompt that people put plates of food on their doorstep for him to eat with confidence he would be there shortly. Leather Man rarely entered a home or accepted shelter in a barn or outbuilding. The many caves he lodged in are woven through the Connecticut and New York countryside and are now revered as attractions for the adventurous who retrace his steps through the region. It was in these caves that he kept his meager belongings—handmade beds, some smoking pipes, a few utensils and perhaps a book or two.

As time went by, it became an honor to have the legendary figure stop at one's doorstep, grunting for a refreshment. He never sought repair for his clothing, always mending it himself with pieces of boot leather he would find, which means he was probably efficient in leather work. He was known for his appetite, as records from one store indicate he procured a loaf of bread, a can of sardines, crackers, pie, two quarts of coffee, a gill of brandy and a bottle of beer. Where he obtained the funds to pay for this or if he actually ever needed to acquire money is forever a mystery. As to his timely circuit, the Darrow family of Shrub Oak in northern Westchester, New York, kept an account of the Leather Man's visits to the hamlet. From 1885 to 1889, he passed through town every thirty-four days on the dot. This he did 360 times for thirty-nine towns in his thirty years of roaming the countryside.

Leather Man died on March 24, 1889, in a Saw Mill Woods cave in Sing-Sing, New York. Some records say it was from a fall, but popular consensus states that it was from the mouth and throat cancer he refused treatment for. In his bag were found leather-working equipment such as scissors, awls, wedges, a small axe and a prayer book written in French. An Englishman

A rare postcard photo of the Leather Man. *From the authors' collection.*

named Sampson Fiske-King Bennett soon came forward, claiming to have spent time with Bourglay in Ninevah, Paris and Ur. The French gentleman paid for Bourglay's burial in Sparta Cemetery in Westchester, New York. A post marked the burial site until the 1930s, when the Westchester Historical Society placed a proper stone over the grave. The stone read, "Final Resting Place of Jules Bourglay of Lyons, France 'The Leather Man' who regularly walked a 365-mile route through Westchester and Connecticut from the Connecticut River to the Hudson, living in caves, in the years 1858–1889."

In 2012, an attempt was made to disinter the remains of the Leather Man and perform DNA tests to find out who he actually was. The old and mysterious itinerant was not about to be outdone. When his grave was exhumed, there remained very little evidence of someone ever being buried there and certainly nothing to take a sample from. The dirt and pieces of coffin or whatever was left were reburied deeper in the cemetery under a stone that simply states, "The Leather Man."

## Cling Clang

Deep in the recesses of Maine's history lies an interesting tale of a peddler who roamed the countryside selling his wares while fixing clocks and tinware. Peddlers were commonplace in early New England, where stores were scarce and many goods unavailable in certain regions. The traveling purveyor of wares was often a welcome sight for the villagers who found need for a new item or repair for an existing relic. Some used carts to transport their goods, while others carried cumbersome sacks on their backs, often using walking sticks for aid of travel.

The peddler usually had a small country store somewhere in the region as his main point of operation. He would make his rounds from town to town before returning home to tend to business at his permanent mercantile establishment. Soon enough, he would head back out on the road to deal his wares to the wanting folk of the region.

Others lived on the road, selling and trading goods for their daily sustenance. Such was the way of the main character in this narrative, a man called Cling Clang by those who knew him.

The one thing that made Cling Clang stand out literally above his peers was the way he traveled from town to town. Cling Clang did not walk like the rest of his profession; instead, he used two large poles with brass tips to vault across the countryside. Traveling through the coastal towns of Maine and occasionally crossing into New Hampshire or Nova Scotia, Cling was able to bound ten to twelve feet at a time, leaping over ditches, brush and fences with the greatest of ease. He derived his name from the way his wares would clank together with each vault, making a clinging and clanging in his pack. His arrival was easily detected from afar by the distinct noise he and his merchandise created, but there was more to the peculiar character than his way of travel.

Cling fashioned his own clothing from old sacks and rags he found along his routes. They were not very fashionable to the eye, but they served him well, as he could stretch his arms or legs to make the most of his vaulting with ease. In the colder months, he would use old sacks to create a primitive sort of footwear. An awesome sight he must have been racing down the road with his long, streaky hair flowing upward behind him with each vault.

Cling was a clean individual, despite his choice of garb. He would take pains to bathe and wash his clothes in a river or stream every few days. This made him more accepted than other peddlers of the time, and he was often invited to join families for supper while passing through. His manner of repast was also rather odd. He would separate his meal and consume each course individually. When one part of his meal was consumed, he eagerly partook in the next course. If gravy was served, he placed it aside and drank it separately. He would eat the bread or biscuit and then eat the butter. The same applied to his coffee or tea. First, he imbibed the liquid plain and afterward ate two spoonfuls of sugar. When supper was over, the family would offer him a bed for the night, but old Cling would reach into his sack, pull out a barrel head and point to the shed or barn. The barrel head served as his pillow, and it served him well each night, for he slept like a baby except when a rooster crowed. Cling had some odd aversion to the sound of a rooster crowing. When he stayed at a farm, he would kindly request the owners put the roosters in for the night.

An archaic account is related from an incident at Swan's Island when a few mischievous lads let a rooster out very early in the morning while Cling was slumbering. The rooster let out his morning alarm, and Cling came dashing out of the shed, mounted his poles and flew at breakneck speed from the farm as if it meant his life. He never returned to that vicinity again.

Cling Clang finally met his end on a harsh winter night in Sullivan, Maine. He stopped at a home to sell his wares, had supper and left to parts unknown. A few locals searched for him and found him under an overturned boat, frozen to death with his fingers still clutching his barrel head. The good folk of Sullivan buried the vaulting peddler, but his legend will forever leap in the annals of Maine's most interesting characters. The only sad part is no one ever knew his real name.

# They Dared Great Things

## John Hays Hammond Jr.

John Hays Hammond Jr. was born in 1888. He later moved from his San Francisco home, wandering about taking on several occupations. His most important decision would be settling in Washington, D.C., as an employee of the U.S. Patent Office. It was there that he received his inspiration to invent. In 1914, he invented a forty-four-foot radio-controlled ship that made a 120-mile round trip from his home to Boston and back with no one to pilot the vessel, only his hands working a remote control he invented. He went on to patent many more inventions. He would soon become friends with Alexander Graham Bell and Thomas Edison, the only other inventor to have more patents than Hammond at the time.

In 1926, he began to build a castle in Gloucester, Massachusetts, to house his great collection of Roman, Medieval and Renaissance artifacts. By 1929, Hammond and his wife, Irene, were settled into their eclectic estate, showing off their collections to anyone who wished to tour the castle.

Hammond was also a believer in the paranormal and reincarnation. The couple's love for cats led him to believe he would come back as a feline when his mortal tenure as a human being had ceased. Hammond was among the many inventors who took deep interest in attempting to successfully communicate with the dead. He invented several machines in an attempt to make contact with the other side of the veil. One of those machines was a Faraday cage he constructed between 1956 and 1957 to test if a medium was authentic. A certain current would pass through the cage, but only a true psychic would feel the current, as it was allegedly a pulse from another world. The cage was cumbersome, and its use left burn marks in the floor of the Great Hall, where they still exist today.

Irene Hammond died in 1959 at the castle and was buried in her family plot. John followed in 1965, but he was buried in the mausoleum beside his grand palace. Along with him were entombed several of his beloved cats that had passed away and were embalmed. In 2008, the museum moved his body to the garden, selling the mausoleum and land it sat on for upkeep of the castle.

It soon became evident that perhaps, true to his word, he had returned as a cat. Shortly after his death, a black cat showed up at the castle and took to the home as if he had lived there his whole life. The kitty instinctively knew the layout of the castle and seemed to enjoy time in the same rooms and areas Mr. Hammond found joy in. The feline was particularly fond of nestling in Mr. Hammond's favorite chair, just as the inventor did when he was in human form.

As time rolled on, the cat passed away, but soon after, another mysteriously showed up in its place. Just like the previous, the cat was already familiar with the castle and grounds. This has been the routine at the castle that also holds the spirit of his wife and a few other ghosts. Not only did he possibly create an energy field that allowed his wife and others to return, it seems that John Hays Hammond Jr., master of 800-plus inventions and holder of 435 patents, found a way to eternally regenerate his soul in the form of his favorite fur creature: a cat.

# WILLIAM MILLER

On October 22, 1844, over one million people gathered on hills, mountaintops and inside cemeteries singing hymns and praying out loud while waiting the midnight tolling. It was that moment, they were told, that the Great Reckoning would commence. The sky was to burst open, and all the true followers were to be whisked up to heaven, leaving the rest of humanity to die by fire.

These ardent followers sold all their belongings, destroyed their homes and threw their money and valuables aside for the greedy and the damned to gather. They were known as "Millerites," led by one man who proclaimed to have received a message from God directing him to tell the world of the second coming.

William Miller was born in Pittsfield, Massachusetts, in 1782. He became a bright young lad, learning much about many things, including religion. He later joined the army, where he received a leg injury. While riding to the hospital, he fell out of the cart onto his head, suffering a brain trauma. This would perhaps play a role in his destiny as a self-ordained savior. During and after his tenure in the military, he studied the Bible enthusiastically, looking for the exact date of Judgment Day. Basing mathematical calculations on scriptures, he concluded that Judgment Day would occur between March 21, 1843, and March 21, 1844.

His first message came in 1831, when he claimed God told him to let the world know of the final judgment. Having no way to tell the masses, he was told, "That will be arranged." As if some miracle had transpired, a messenger arrived at his door informing Miller the local preacher had taken ill and requested he perform the Sabbath sermon in the morning.

He began his crusade warning the populace about the Day of Reckoning. He instructed the congregation to look for four signs.

1. Wonders would be seen in the skies.
2. The earth would tremble and shake in various places throughout the world.
3. There would be war among man.
4. Man would show marked intelligence in earthly progress.

Either by coincidence or divine intervention, the signs began to appear. On November 13, 1833, thousands of brilliant lights fell from the sky and balls of fire could be seen in the north for almost an hour. Soon it was reported that earthquakes had taken place in England, India and the West Indies. Industrial expansion and inventions were now taking place, and of course, there were wars and revolutions.

Millerites spread across the nation, and William Miller traveled everywhere delivering speeches and sermons to the crowds of followers. Time was drawing nearer to the hour when another spectacular show took place in the skies. The people feared their time was close. They gathered in camps, taking loved ones who had recently passed with them so they may ascend to heaven as well. Some killed their whole families and then committed suicide, believing that the dead would enter heaven first. Women refused to marry, as they wished to enter heaven as virgins. One woman declared she was in personal contact with the Savior and was instructed to walk across a river in proof of his association with her. She drowned. A man claimed he had the powers of flight and drove his buggy over a cliff, where he met the most awful fate as he crashed into the rocks below.

When the Great Comet of 1843 passed overhead, even the most stout Christian began to doubt his faith and turned into a Millerite. Miller published an announcement in the *New York Herald* that the Day of Judgment was April 3. Flocks of followers gathered in droves, singing and praising their savior while waiting for their glorious moment of ascension. April 3 came and went without fire and brimstone. The Millerites, undaunted, concluded that the day would still fall between March 1843 and March 1844. When March 21, 1844, arrived, the flock once again took their positions on the hilltops, chanting and praying. Many once again committed suicide or burned all their earthly possessions. Slowly, the sun rose as the day of March 22 began without fanfare. The Millerites, with nowhere to go, were crushed by their foolish behavior, but William Miller had one more consolation for them. He confided that he had used the Gregorian calendar instead of the Hebrew one; therefore, his calculations were off by several months. A message was sent to all the churches stating, "I humbly announce as a faithful Disciple, that the Second Advent of Christ will occur October 22, 1844. Prepare yourself for this Great Day!"

The Millerites reconvened, adding more to their numbers. The new date came, and once again, the faithful millions gathered in high places awaiting their ascension. A farmer in Chester, Vermont, had special "Ascension" robes made for his best cows with the notion that they would be "mighty handy up there," as the children would need milk after the long journey.

The night came and went like any other previously, and the morning found the groups still awaiting their ascension into heaven. This time, they would walk off the mountains and hills complete paupers, as they had destroyed or sold all their worldly possessions. Thousands of suicides took place. In many cases, whole families took their own lives. Hospitals and asylums were overrun by the distraught and depressed. Despite the suffering Miller caused, he lived comfortably on his stately farm until his death in 1849. The man who saw the end gave it to many people, but not the way they had hoped. They had come to believe they would hear the triumphant voices from beyond, calling them to heaven, but instead, they only heard one man's crazed prophecy.

# THE GHOST OF THE WHITE BIRD

Charles Lindbergh is well known in history for the first transatlantic flight after leaving Long Island, New York, on May 20, 1927, and landing safely in Paris, France, on May 21, thirty-three and one-half hours and thirty-six thousand miles later. A lesser-known legacy is that of two pilots who took off from a Paris airfield and crossed the Atlantic Ocean twelve days before. The only difference—they never reached their final destination.

On May 8, 1927, *L'Oiseau Blanc*, or the White Bird, left Le Bouget airfield in Paris en route to New York. The Levasseur PL.8 aircraft was propelled by a 450-horsepower Lorraine-Dietrich twelve-cylinder water-cooled engine and held three fuel tanks totaling 1,100 gallons, which would give them forty-two hours of flight time—more than enough to complete their purpose. The PL.8 also incorporated small floats attached directly to the undersides of the lower wing. The landing gear could be jettisoned on takeoff in order to reduce the aircraft's weight. The underside of the fuselage was given a boat-like shape and made watertight for a water landing, as the two planned on landing in New York Harbor, in front of the Statue of Liberty.

The pilot, Charles Nungesser, was a decorated World War I flying ace, and navigator Francois Coli had several successful flights under his belt. The two wore specially designed flying suits for the long journey over the Atlantic.

A 1927 postcard of *L'Oiseau Blanc* (the White Bird) and its two ill-fated pilots. *Photo by Arlene Nicholson from the authors' collection.*

The biplane left the airfield at 5:41 a.m., barely clearing the treetops due to its cumbersome size and weight.

The plane was seen flying overhead a small town in Ireland before heading out over the Atlantic. No further sightings were reported. On May 9, people in New York awaited the arrival of the White Bird, but after it failed to show, everyone feared the plane had met with disaster. The White Bird and its crew, as Lindbergh later stated, "vanished like midnight ghosts."

According to witnesses in Newfoundland, the aircraft was sighted over a dozen times. On May 9 at 9:20 a.m., Arthur Doyle and three other eyewitnesses spied a white biplane coming off the Atlantic toward land. Just after 10:00 a.m., several more witnesses saw the plane pass over Harbor Grace. Airplanes were rare at that time, so the sight of one was certainly memorable. Sometime in the early afternoon, Anson Berry reported hearing a low-flying plane crash near his camp at Round Lake in Maine. He also stated that just before the crash, the engine was sputtering erratically. Searches for the missing plane turned up nothing, and the matter was left to legend until 1980, when Gunner Hanson, better known as Leatherface in the movie *Texas Chainsaw Massacre*, took interest in the story.

Hanson spoke with a hunter who, in 1950, had discovered a large engine partially buried in the woods of Maine where the plane had reportedly crashed. Subsequent searches for the wreckage turned up pieces of struts and engine parts but little else. The plane, being mostly constructed of wood, would have long rotted away.

Another clue that would lead to a dead end for the discovery of the aircraft's remains turned up when locals remembered that a large engine was dragged from the woods during a logging operation in 1974 and sold for scrap.

Lindbergh may have been correct in his statement, but in a more supernatural manner. Although the White Bird may never be physically identified, its ghostly visitations are a different story. On the anniversary of the plane's disappearance, the woods take on a more ominous tone, and the sounds of the White Bird are once again heard. Witnesses near Round Lake hear the eerie sound of a very low-flying aircraft and have actually witnessed the trees part as if something was brushing their tops. Some claim to hear a crash but, upon investigating, find no sign of any such tragedy. Perhaps it is the ghosts of Coli and Nungesser reliving that fateful moment when they touched down on American soil but never lived to celebrate their accomplishment.

# HIRAM MARBLE

In 1658, a major earthquake shook New England, causing much terror and distress to its people. One other interesting note in the history of the region took place in Lynn, Massachusetts, where a pirate named Thomas Veal was said to have resided in a cave among Lynn Woods' thicket. The pirate had arrived sometime before with a small band and managed to evade capture when the British found their hideout. He came to the cave in the woods and there made his home. Of course, his comrades were not so fortunate. It is told that Veal also took with him a vast treasure and hid the cache in the cave, where he lived under the light of pine knots until that fateful day in 1658 when the quake sealed Veal and his treasure under the great rock.

Time passed and tales were told, but few dared to excavate the cave where the pirate and his treasure lay for centuries. Even the famous Moll Pitcher spoke of the riches that lay buried underneath the tons of rock but never made any attempt to search for it. Then came a man led by spirits to the great rock and the treasure that lay within.

Hiram Marble, an ardent spiritualist from Charlton, Massachusetts, received messages from the other side informing him he would soon find a vast treasure hidden somewhere. The message was to the effect that he would find the riches along with the bones of a pirate. He heard about the rock and its story and immediately followed his preordained destiny. After purchasing the rock and five surrounding acres in 1852, he and his family set up a home and began to blast at the massive boulder. This occurred during the fledgling stages of the Spiritualist movement that had taken the world by storm. There were plenty of mediums in every community to consult, which Marble did on his every move. One particular medium, Nancy Snow Emerson, became his regular channel to the other world, so much so that he wrote a book, *The History of Dungeon Rock*, based on the perspective of the ghostly words that spewed from her mouth during séances. The book, with the name ENESEE on the cover, is a pseudonym for Nancy S. Emerson.

At first, enthusiasm ran high, but the rock fought back with its impenetrable face. Progress was slow, and daily blasting and carrying the rubble by buckets often only amounted to one foot per month leeway into the giant boulder. The consultations with the medium were constant, as she voiced the will of Thomas Veal. The direction of the cave as it began to take shape often took sharp rights and lefts. No matter what the spirit wished, Marble heeded for fear of losing the presence of the ghost of Veal or, worse, the treasure. Soon another pirate spirit came into the picture, that of Captain Harris. Both were in contact with Marble throughout his ordeal. One example of his conversations with the pirate ghosts is as follows. Marble would write on a piece of paper his request, and it would be answered in automatic writing. Here is an account of one of the séances.

"I wish Veal or Harris would tell what move to make next."

Marble then covered the statement with fifteen other pieces of parchment. The medium only needed to lay her clairvoyant hand on the top piece and she would become entranced by the pirate ghosts. This is what was answered:

> *Dear Charge, you solicit me or Captain Harris to advise you as to what to next do. Well, as Harris says he has always had the heft of the load on his shoulders, I will try and respond myself and let Harris rest. Ha! ha! Well, Marble, we must joke a bit; did we not, we should have the blues, as do you some of those rainy days when you see no living person at the rock, save your own dear ones. Not a sound do you hear, save the woodpecker and that little gray bird* [Marble's pet canary], *that sings all day long, more especially wet days, tittry, tittry, tittry. But, Marble, as Long* [a deceased friend of Marble] *says, don't be discouraged. We are doing as fast as we can. As to the course, you are in the right direction at present. You have one more curve to make before you take the course that leads to the cave. We have a reason for keeping you from entering the cave at once. Moses was by the Lord kept forty years in his circuitous route, ere he had sight of that land that flowed with milk and honey. God had his purpose in so doing, not withstanding he might have led Moses into the promise, in a very few days from the start. But no; God wanted to develop a truth, and no faster than the minds of the people were prepared to receive it. Cheer up, Marble, we are with you and doing all we can.*
> *Your guide,*
> *TOM VEAL.*

As funds grew low, Marble sold bonds and gave tours of the cave that now spiraled deep into the rock. For twenty-five cents, one could enter past the grated iron door that covered the cave entrance and descend toward the depths of what would be known as Dungeon Rock. On the door was a sign that stated, "Ye who enter here, leave twenty-five cents behind."

Marble set up a visitor center where he displayed the notes and drawings that came from the mediums during their trances. Also displayed were pieces of iron, one resembling the remains of a sword scabbard, some odd but captivating stones and plans for a Spiritualist center that was to be built

Hiram Marble's stone in Bay Path
Cemetery, Charlton, Massachusetts.

with some of the riches. The scabbard was reportedly discovered wedged between two stones during excavation. An amusing note on the scabbard lies within the pages of Samuel Adams Drake's *A Book of New England Legends and Folklore*, where Drake later mentions the scabbard during a tour of Dungeon Rock to Longfellow, who, in return, tells Drake that he remembers seeing the same artifact years before in a blacksmith shop.

After sixteen years of excavating at the rock, Hiram Marble died on September 10, 1868, and was buried in the cemetery near the common of Charlton. His son Edwin continued his father's work while keeping in contact with the spirits on every move until he, too, passed away in 1880. Unlike his father, Edwin did not wish to be buried in Charlton but chose instead to be buried next to the cave he so laboriously excavated for most of his life. The large pink boulder near the entrance of the cave marks Edwin's final resting place. Both of them had tunneled a total of two hundred feet into the great boulder, zigzagging into the earth on the orders of the spirits, yet never discovered the location of the treasure that so eluded them. Hiram Marble dreamed of using the cache to buy more of the land he lived on and turn it into a public park for all to enjoy.

In a twist of fate, the land, now called Lynn Woods, became the second-largest municipal park in the United States. Countless people hike the trails and take in the bountiful nature the park affords. Most take time to stop at the grated iron door Hiram Marble placed in front of the cave entrance to protect his claim. When the door is unlocked, visitors may descend the wooden steps into the fissure that winds back and forth, sometimes but a few feet tall but mostly negotiable.

The remains of Hiram Marble's home sit but a few yards from the entrance of Dungeon Rock. Both are the remnants of a lasting testament to the two men who, on the words of a pirate's spirit, spent their lives blasting away at a chunk of stone.

# Dr. Thomas Benton

The White Mountains afford the most beautiful scenery in the region. Whether driving the winding back roads, hiking the trails or visiting the many natural wonders, the area is a must-visit. The perennial peaks are always joyous to behold. Another perennial figure is also still seen along the peaks and fissures near Benton, New Hampshire, a man named Dr. Thomas Benton. What makes the appearance of Dr. Benton so terrifying is that he was born in the 1800s.

As a young man, Thomas dreamed of practicing medicine. Having no other professional doctor in the region, the community came together and funded his education on the stipulation that he would return to become the town's first and only doctor. Benton studied medicine in Germany, where he became close friends with Dr. Stockmayer, a man who was working on a bizarre medical experiment. When Benton returned to his home, he brought with him a trunk. Its contents were believed to contain everything needed to complete Stockmayer's experiments for an elixir of youth.

Thomas soon fell in love with a beautiful young woman, and they engaged to marry. All seemed to be going well for the young doctor until his fiancée died of typhoid fever. The tragic death of his love took its toll on Benton's mental capacity, and he stole away to the mountains, where he built a cabin on the top of Mount Moosilauke.

Not long after the doctor went into seclusion, local farmers noticed that their livestock disappeared or died under mysterious circumstances. The farmers discovered a peculiar red swelling with a white pinprick behind each animal's left ear. They feared it might be the work of the elusive doctor performing bizarre experiments on their animals.

Some local farmers gathered up their courage and decided to question the doctor regarding their livestock's strange disappearances and deaths. Together they ascended the mountain, hoping to find out once and for all what the doctor was doing. The throng knocked on the door, but their raps were met with silence. The door swung open, revealing strange apparatus and the remnants of some recent experiment but no doctor. They began to descend the peak as darkness set in, causing one of the men to become separated from the rest. The next day, they found the poor soul dead. The only mark on him was the familiar swelling and pinprick behind his left ear.

It was not long before the doctor decided to test his experiments on human subjects. Babies began mysteriously disappearing from their cradles in the dead of night. Suspicion immediately fell on Dr. Benton, although there was no physical proof until one day, a woman was in her yard when a man with long white hair and a black cloak ran up to her young daughter and snatched her away into the woods. A band of men led by the daughter's father followed the footprints in the snow along Tunnel Ravine to a cliff. There they spied Thomas Benton high above them on a ledge. The party demanded he release the girl forthwith, which he did to the ravages of the rocks below. After that heinous act, Benton was never seen again.

In 1860, the Prospect House was built on the summit of Mount Moosilauke. Visitors and tourists at first shied from the house for fear of an evil Dr. Benton encounter. Their fears were substantiated when a cable that secured the house was cut by hand. A logger volunteered to repair the truss but never returned. They found him dead a short time later, with the telltale red swelling and pinprick behind his left ear.

By 1881, the building was expanded and renamed the Tip Top House. People began flocking to the mountain retreat, confident that Dr. Benton was now long passed. This feeling of security was short-lived when reports began to circulate of a dark shadow in a cloak seen slinking among the trees.

The house became abandoned for some time until Charles and E.K. Woodworth purchased the building and then donated it to Dartmouth College in a twist of fate. By 1920, the Dartmouth Outdoor Club owned a portion of the mountain and ran the house as an Appalachian Mountain Club hut. It burned down in 1942, but the stone foundation remains. A building was constructed near the site and exists today in the style and atmosphere of years past.

Sightings of a mysterious dark form roaming around the mountaintop in old colonial-style clothing are still reported to this day. In 2003, while taking a short rest, a hiker found an old-style boot print in the mud near the summit of Mount Moosilauke. Not only was the print that of a century-old boot, but it also was not on the trail moments before. Some swear they have seen the shape of Dr. Benton as it bounds through the thicket. Those who believe it is Dr. Benton claim that he has not aged a day in centuries. If it is the evil doctor, he may have found the secret of eternal life and is now a hermit of the mountains.

Mount Moosilauke is located between Benton and North Woodstock.

# D.D. Home

In 1848, an event transpired that would change the way many thought about the afterlife. The Fox sisters of Hydesville, New York, became subject to the knocking and rapping of what was considered incarnate souls. The Spiritualist movement was born and continued well into the twentieth century. Mediums, mostly charlatans, seized the opportunity to make a living by conjuring ways to create stimuli and visual effects during séances. People paid dearly for the chance to speak with their loved ones on the other side. Inspired by the new Spiritualist movement, many divination forms became popular for communication with the other side, including the Ouija board. During this time, a man named Daniel Dunglas Home (pronounced Hume) came into the public eye.

Daniel Dunglas Home was born in Scotland in 1833. He came to America with his aunt and uncle at the age of nine. His parents and other siblings soon joined them. They settled in Norwich, Connecticut, and began a new life the American way. However, something was off. Daniel was not like the other children. Even at his young age, he showed signs of strange abilities he later claimed he inherited from his mother. As he grew older, these abilities increased.

Daniel made a pact with his childhood friend, promising that if there were a way to communicate after death, the first one to die would do so to the other. One night, Daniel had a vision of his friend, who was in good health when he last visited. The vision showed his friend had died from a sudden illness. A few days later, news came of the abrupt demise of the friend.

When Daniel's mother died in 1849, the event was followed by rapping and knocking on the aunt's house's wall where he resided. Being pious, the aunt thought it the work of the devil and threw a chair at Daniel. At that moment, other pieces of furniture began to move about the house and continued every time Daniel was present until he was sent away for good.

Everywhere Daniel went, rapping, furniture moving and what appeared to be shadows of the dead followed him. Newspapers got wind of this unusual phenomenon and swept right in, making him a celebrity in the Spiritualist community. One particular account transpired in March 1851, when Home conducted a séance. A table thrust itself into the air in front of the witnesses and moved without any living person's assistance. Then, at the participants' request, it flipped itself over and came to rest in the laps of the group.

Home considered his talents a gift from God and began to use them for the good of his fellow man. People from all walks of life flocked to the seer for help in every way possible. Home never charged for his services, although he did receive gifts and donations that allowed him to live a comfortable life. He held séances sometimes several times a day, relaying messages from the dead through knocking and rapping while furniture slid about the room.

One of the most notable events took place in the home of Manchester, Connecticut resident Ward Cheney. A man named Franklin Burr was present, along with several other men. Burr's brother, the editor of the *Hartford Daily Times*, was also in attendance.

While blindfolded, Home spelled out messages from the dead by pointing to the letters on a card. Rapping on the table signaled when the word was complete. Suddenly, there was the sound of a ship caught in a fierce storm. Flapping of sails was heard and the creaking and groaning resembling a ship under stress from the storm. Communication came through from two relatives of one of the men present at the séance. They were sailors lost at sea. The scene became more dramatic when the table, weighing about one hundred pounds, suddenly rose from the floor. Burr jumped on the table, but it rose again, rocking back and forth. It finally tilted to one side, sliding Burr off.

Another member of the group leaped on the table but met the same fate as Burr. The sufficiently lighted room proved trickery was not involved. The men could see over the table and under, and there was nothing beneath the table. Burr later reported that Home was suddenly lifted from his seat without warning and levitated approximately a foot above the chair. Home himself was as stunned as the rest of the men. He was lifted three separate times that night; the third time, his head and hands gently touched the ceiling. The witnesses, feeling around his feet and body, could find no wire or any other form of trickery to account for the phenomenon. The spirits had upped their game with Home from simple furniture moving to levitation.

In 1855, Home left for England on his doctor's request, for he had contracted consumption, the nineteenth-century term for tuberculosis. Home never returned to the United States, but he did become a celebrity in Europe, performing séances for everyone who asked, including royalty, often levitating for them. Home died in 1886, but his legacy has survived to this day, as no one has ever been able to disprove his abilities. Magicians of today can only suggest how he may have achieved this "trick," but everyone who ever sat in a room with Home attested that there was no form of trickery whatsoever.

# CAPTAIN THUNDERBOLT

Many may not be familiar with the term "highwayman." It has been centuries since the last of these bold bandits roamed the roads and trails of early America. Men and women were well aware of the dangers of traveling alone, for many a robber awaited in the brush for an ill-gained bounty. The last of the highwaymen came to be when Michael Martin, alias Captain Lightfoot, swung from the gallows in 1821. His partner, Captain Thunderbolt, was known to have met the same fate several years before in Ireland—or did he?

When teacher and physician John Wilson arrived in Brattleboro, Vermont, the people welcomed him. His charming manners, skill with medicine and ability to train the young in both manners and education were needed assets for the town. Wilson owned several properties in the county that he began to sell for one reason or another before finally settling in Brattleboro. The accounts of his medical training range from the University in Edinburgh, Scotland, to classes at the Academy of Medicine in Castleton, Vermont.

Wilson took over the practice of Dr. John Morse, who died in 1822, at the request of a few friends and colleagues. Dr. Wilson made many friends during his life in Windham County, so much so that no one later could fathom what was about to unfold after his death.

John Wilson died on March 22, 1847, after suffering four days with acute erysipelas, a form of cellulitis. Upon preparing his body for burial, several strange things came to light. It was discovered that the doctor had rope burns on his neck, which explained why he always wore a cravat or scarf of some sort. There was a wound resembling a musket shot removed by primitive surgery. Wilson also had a portion of his heel missing. His shoe was packed to conceal the wound and help him walk without a severe limp. Several other strange wounds were discovered that did not match up to the life of an educator or medical physician.

The scars and wounds were too much to send quietly to the grave. Word got out, and it was not long before someone came forward with a startling revelation after having read the life and confession of Michael Martin, alias Captain Lightfoot. Dr. Wilson was none other than Martin's mentor and partner in crime, Captain Thunderbolt. The wounds mirrored the descriptions Martin gave in his memoir

Captain Thunderbolt. *From the authors' collection.*

128

that his partner, Thunderbolt, had sustained during their exploits. In a letter recounted in Martin's confession, the writer describes what Wilson looked like during the autopsy:

> *The calf of his leg was perished that he wore a cork heel—that he had been considerably wounded in the neck, as it was much scarified—and also true that he would not suffer, in his last sickness, his clothes to be taken off, save his coat—not even his handkerchief. I never, to my recollection, saw him without a handkerchief about his neck, and that, too, a large one. If the weather was ever so hot, a thick heavy muffler was invariably about his neck. His perished limb was kept out to the size of the other by wadding made of paper. How he could have always concealed his lameness from everybody, is odd enough; and why he should have concealed it, is somewhat of a puzzle.*

Wilson lacked medical licenses or certificates of graduation from appropriate institutions that other physicians proudly displayed on the walls of their offices. For those who may have wondered why, the answer was now clear. It was most likely to escape any public scrutiny. This bewildering discovery did very little to dissuade many who thought of the man as an able-bodied, educated physician and colleague. Dr. Cyrus Washburn of Vernon, Vermont, wrote of his character:

> *Dr. Wilson, the famous "Thunderbolt," who lived in Brattleboro after a life as a highway robber, had not only the tolerance but the respect of Dr. Washburn. While other physicians would not recognize the man without his showing a certificate of some kind, Dr. Washburn recognized him by his ability to do good work. It is probable that the fugitive from justice was the ablest physician in the state at the time.*

Was Dr. John Wilson actually the famous Captain Thunderbolt who figured so prominently in Michael Martin's 1821 confession? The evidence seems to point toward the affable doctor once leading a life of lawlessness and intemperance. After he was buried, found among his earthly possessions were two double-barreled guns; two pairs of horse pistols; two or three dueling pistols; a number of swords, one of which had a steel network to secure the hand; and a dozen walking canes of all sorts and sizes. One contained inside a sort of ramrod, which, by pointing the cane toward anyone and giving it a slight jerk, would make a noise similar to the cocking of a gun. He also left quite a variety of powder horns, shot bags and bullet pouches.

The weather-worn stone of Dr. John Wilson, alias Captain Thunderbolt.

One more small tidbit to ponder: Wilson owned two steam mills, one in Newfane and the other in Williamsville, Vermont. He also was credited with designing a round schoolhouse during a small tenure as a teacher in Brookline, Vermont. The schoolhouse is now a famous historical landmark in the town.

## THE LUCREZIA BORGIA OF ANSONIA

This story is told with kind thanks to Ansonia native author and historian John William Tuohy.

During the height of her fame, Lydia Sherman was dubbed "America's Queen Killer," "The Poison Fiend," "The Modern-Day Lucrezia Borgia" and "The Derby Poisoner." The *New York Times* called Lydia Sherman the "Lucrezia Borgia" of Ansonia. Still, she was actually far worse, having poisoned at least eleven people, probably more, before she died in Wethersfield State Prison in 1878. Eight of the people she killed were children in her care, six of whom were her own, along with her three husbands.

Sherman was born Lydia Danbury in New Jersey in 1824 and raised by an uncle. At age sixteen, she went to work as a tailor. A year later, she met and married Edward Struck, a widower with two children and a policeman in Yorkville, New York.

Portrait of Lydia Sherman, circa 1870. *Courtesy of the New England Historical Society.*

Seven years went by, and the couple had six children together. Struck lost his job (a detective was killed "in a row in a saloon" when Struck was supposed to be on duty but was away without leave and subsequently fired) and fell into a deep depression. Lydia poisoned him by mixing a "thimbleful" of arsenic into his oatmeal gruel, and after several hours of vomiting, abdominal pain, diarrhea and convulsions, Edward died. Within weeks Lydia, now working as a nurse, killed their three youngest children. By the end of the year, she succeeded in murdering her remaining three children, all by poison.

In 1867, Lydia took a nursing job in Stratford and met and married Dennis Hurlburt, a

The arrest of Lydia Sherman. *From the authors' collection.*

wealthy Litchfield farmer and fisherman. He was much older than Lydia, something she probably planned since Mr. Hurlburt "possessed very few attractions, besides his property." Shortly after their marriage, Hurlburt changed his will, leaving everything to Lydia.

Without warning, he grew ill and died suddenly, leaving Lydia his $30,000 estate, equal to about half a million in today's dollars. A respectable middle-class income of the time was $2,000 a year. Yet no one suspected anything unusual.

Only eight weeks later, she went to work as a housekeeper in Ansonia, then a part of Derby called Birmingham, for a widower and father of two named Horatio N. Sherman. Within a few weeks of working for Sherman, Lydia married him. Within a short time, Sherman's infant son fell ill and died for reasons unknown. Then Sherman's teenage daughter became sick and died, and finally, Sherman himself followed close behind.

A local Ansonia, Yale-trained doctor named Beardsley was suspicious and ordered an autopsy, which disclosed the use of poison. Beardsley then authorized the bodies of Sherman's children to be exhumed, as well as Dennis Hurlburt's body. An examination of the bodies proved all three were poisoned.

In the meantime, Lydia fled the city but was arrested in June 1871 for the murder of Horatio N. Sherman.

She was tried in New Haven in 1872. She contended in her defense that she accidentally killed Sherman but did intend to murder his children. She claimed Sherman ingested the arsenic, believing it was saleratus, a baking soda–like compound that, when mixed with cider, made it foam. Doctors agreed Sherman appeared to have mistakenly mixed the arsenic that his wife had bought to kill him and his children with a cider glass.

The jury found her guilty of second-degree murder. A while later, in 1873, she made a full confession, admitting to poisoning her "three husbands and four children." On January 11, 1873, Judge Sanford of New Haven sentenced Lydia Sherman to life in Wethersfield State Prison.

On June 5, 1877, Sherman escaped from Wethersfield, making her way to Rhode Island, where she checked into a Providence hotel using the name "Mrs. Brown." No one suspected her until she made the grave error of referring to herself by a different last name. Suspicious, the hotel keeper called the police, and they arrested Sherman.

A while later, a surprise inspection of Sherman's cell revealed

> *a piece of crayon of a very "bilious" color, believed that the woman, as a "crayon artiste," has for a long time made a complexion to and from experimenting with it upon the white skin of different persons it was found that a little brisk rubbing would change the color of the cuticle from a clear white to a sickly yellow: and it is now suit the demands of an artificial fever complaint and make prison life endurable.*

Lydia Sherman died a year later, on May 16, 1878, after several weeks of illness, probably from cancer, at age fifty-one. She remained famous even after her demise. In 1873 and 1878, two different companies published her 1873 confession.

# From Beyond the Grave

## The Vengeful Ghost of Rebecca Cornell

Do you believe that the spirit of someone can come back to avenge their death? In 1673, the people of Portsmouth, Rhode Island, became convinced that Rebecca Cornell's ghost helped solve her own murder. The court of Portsmouth recorded the case with acute accuracy.

Born about 1595 in Essex, England, Thomas Cornell married Rebecca Briggs (born 1600) and came to the New World around 1638. The couple settled in Boston, where he was, by town meeting, permitted to purchase the former property of William Baulstone (Blackstone). He was also granted a permit for an inn. In 1638, Anne Hutchinson and her fellow "Antinomians" were expelled from Puritan Boston. Thomas and his family, along with his brother-in-law John Briggs, were among those who were banished. The small band purchased land from Canonicus and Miantonomi, where they settled on the north of the island, calling it Portsmouth.

The Cornells arrived in Portsmouth on August 6, 1640. In February 1641, Thomas was granted a piece of land and became constable. The spelling "Cornhill" or "Cornell" appears in various old records. Thomas died in 1655, and in about 1657, Rebecca began to both will and divvy out holdings her husband had accrued during his travels in the New World. One of Rebecca's sons, Thomas, and his family lived with her on the Portsmouth farm. For some reason, he did not inherit as much as his siblings. Perhaps

The overgrown Cornell lot on their former property.

it was due to the fact that he was known as being overly idle. Rebecca died tragically one evening, fueling a strange moment in New England history. A curious entry from the Friends Records dated February 8, 1673, states, "Rebecca Cornell, widow, was killed strangely at Portsmouth in her own dwelling house, was twice viewed by the Coroner's Inquest and buried again by her husband's grave in their own land."

The *Arnold Vital Records of Rhode Island 1636–1850*, volume 7, "Friends and Ministers," states on page 96, "Cornell, Rebecca, widow, Portsmouth, killed strangely at her house, February 8, 1673."

On February 8, 1673, Rebecca Cornell was discovered burned to death in her room. The original coroner's inquest, given on February 9, the next day, labeled it as an "unhappie accident of fire," but that would change rather quickly. At the time of the accident, those present believed Mrs. Cornell might have nestled down in her chair by the fire to enjoy smoking her pipe. An ember from the fire or a spark of fire from the pipe somehow ignited her clothes and quickly spread, consuming her in flames. When found, she was barely recognizable.

She was soon buried next to her husband but refused to rest in peace. A few nights later, her brother John Briggs was roused from his sleep by a bright light at the foot of his bed. He immediately recognized it as the glowing countenance of his sister-in-law, Rebecca. She spoke to him, saying, "See how badly I am burned," while exposing a wound in her abdomen.

John Briggs (Brigs), born in Darrington, England, around 1609, married Thomas Cornell Sr.'s sister Sarah, with whom he had six children. Briggs held several important positions in the colonies. His influence would no doubt be instrumental in the trial that would follow. On February 20, 1673, Briggs testified that on February 12, four days after Rebecca had died, he laid in bed and

> *being between sleeping and wakeing, as he thought he felt something heave up the Bedclothes twice, and thought somebody had been coming to bed to him, whereupon he Awaked, and turned himself about in his bed, and being turned, he perceived a light in the roome like to the dawning of ye day, and plainly saw the shape and appearance of a woman standing by his bedside whereat he was much affrighted, and cried out, in the name of God, what art thou, the Apparition answered, I am your sister Cornell, and twice said, see how I was Burnt with fire, and she plainely appeared unto him to be very much burnt about the shoulders, face and head.*

Briggs, thoroughly shaken by the specter, met with the coroner's inquest and demanded a second examination be performed, as he suspected her ghost was insinuating foul play may have contributed to her death. When an autopsy was performed, a wound was present, unseen the first time, showing that she may have met with a more sinister end. The suspicion fell on her son Thomas, who had been in the room with her for roughly one and a half hours on the night she died and was the last to see her alive. An investigation was held, and Thomas was arrested for the murder of his mother. Testimony revealed much about that evening.

Among those examined were Thomas Cornell Jr.; his wife, Sarah; Henry Straight; John Russell; George Soule; James Mills; John Cornell, the son of Thomas and Sarah; and his wife, Mary. Straight was lodging at the Cornell home when the "accident" occurred. He inquired as to why Mrs. Cornell was not at supper, and Thomas told him she cared not for salted mackerel, as it made her dry at night. After dinner, Sarah sent one of the boys to see if his grandmother might want boiled milk for supper. The boy returned, seeking a candle to see what the fire was in the room. The dinner party rushed to the room, and Straight, being the first to enter, saw a fire on the floor and raked it away with his hands. He then noticed the figure on the floor and, thinking it may have been a drunken Indian, began to speak in their language toward the figure. Thomas, recognizing her shoes, cried out, "Oh Lord, it is my mother!"

Straight and the others noticed that the bed curtains and valance were burned but had been put out. He also stated that other times when they had mackerel for supper, Mrs. Cornell would dine with them. James Mills, upon examination, corroborated Straight's testimony.

Thomas Cornell, another son of Thomas and Sarah, testified that he and his father were in the room with Mrs. Cornell the night she died. He left, and his father stayed in the room for about one hour more before coming out to supper, stating that Mrs. Cornell would not be joining them that evening.

Others testified that Thomas and his wife treated the old woman very badly, neglecting her needs and never offering any aid to her. Mary Cornell stated that she once visited the home, where Mrs. Cornell was forced to chase after the pigs as her son offered no help, and that she was weak and tired. She mentioned that she desired to stab a penknife in her heart to end her troubles but chose to "resist ye devil" instead. There was also testimony that she had mentioned being denied food and blankets or a warm fire in the cold of winter. George Soule testified that Mrs. Cornell had told him she was going to go live with her son Samuel come spring if she was not first

The Cornell house. A fire burned much of the original in the late 1800s, but it was rebuilt to be an exact match.

disposed of or made away. She also told Soule there had been a conflict with Thomas about the rent and a hundred-pound bond that Thomas wanted her to forget if he was going to further pay any rent to her.

It was noted that the wool she wore was burned while the cotton clothing was not. Women often wore wool smocks when working near open fires, as wool does not burn but will smolder instead, giving the wearer a chance to shake the smoking vesture.

Based on the testimony of witnesses and neighbors, but mostly on the vision of John Briggs, Thomas Cornell was found guilty of murdering his mother and was sentenced to hang at about one o'clock on May 23, 1673. Cornell did not appeal the sentence but asked permission to be buried next to his mother. The judge denied his request, requiring that he was to be buried in an unmarked grave within twenty feet of the common road.

Thomas's wife was pregnant at the time of his execution, and in protest of his guilty verdict, she named their daughter Innocent. Innocent grew up to be a fine young woman and, in 1691, married a man named Richard Borden. Innocent would become the great-great-great-great-grandmother of Lizzie Borden of Fall River, Massachusetts, who was arrested, tried and acquitted for the August 4, 1892 murders of her father, Andrew, and her stepmother, Abbie Borden.

# A Parrot Once Helped Solve a Triple Murder

In the late nineteenth century, Halifax, Massachusetts, was a close-knit little community of about six hundred people. One journalist in the 1870s referred to the town as such: "no lawyers and none needed." However, that would change on February 15, 1874, when a gruesome triple murder took place in the Sturtevant home.

The elderly two brothers, Simeon and Thomas Sturtevant, lived with their elderly cousin and caretaker, Mercy Buckley. It was well known that they were very wealthy farmers and kept their wealth hidden within the home's confines. Though the neighbors were in the habit of checking on the trio, days would go by where the three would not be seen or heard. On February 16, a neighbor happened to be passing the rear of the home when he noticed Miss Buckley's body lying in a field some forty rods from the house. Her head had been beaten so severely that she was barely recognizable. He hurried to the house, where he found Thomas near the door, also beaten to death. Simeon was found upstairs in the bedroom in the same condition.

The whole community was in utter shock. Right away, the police had a suspect: the nephew of the brothers, William Sturtevant. It was no secret that William owed money and had no means of paying his debts, and his wife had just given birth.

One telltale sign pointing toward his guilt was that a trail of coins leading from the Sturtevant house fell from a hole in his pocket. When the police searched him, they found dollar bills in his stocking issued in 1863—the same ones that the uncles kept in their home. Only a portion of the money was taken, which was also a factor, as William had no way of carrying a large sum; therefore, he would only take what he could fit on his person.

All this was but circumstantial, and although it weighed heavy on the side of justice, it was what happened next that sealed William's fate. The police escorted William to the crime scene for a walk-through. William seemed composed, though nervous, and then it happened. As he passed Buckley's parrot, it began screeching, "Murderer! Murderer!"

William then broke down and confessed to killing his uncles and Buckley with a cart spoke and then taking what he could carry in currency. The trial was so famous that tickets for the event were in high demand. Sturtevant was found guilty and executed on May 7, 1875. A special train was commissioned to bring crowds in to witness the execution. He would be the second to last person executed in Plymouth County.

The two brothers are buried in the Tomson Cemetery in Halifax next to each other. On their stone under their names is the word "Murdered." William is also reported to be buried somewhere in the cemetery in an unmarked grave.

A gruesome story with a strange ending is not uncommon in New England history. This particular one, instead of a copycat murderer, tells of a copycat screaming murder.

# The Seer of Rutland

Chittenden's Eddy family found fame in the well-publicized acts of mediumship and séances in their family home. Only five miles south of the Eddys, another man, Solomon Wright Jewett, was making waves of his own. By the end of the nineteenth century, both parties had put Vermont's otherwise sleepy state on the Spiritualist map.

Jewett was born on May 22, 1808, in Weybridge, Vermont, the seventh son of Samuel and Lucy. He was believed to be born with a "second sight," as his birth took place at a time when all planets but Saturn were ascending. Jewett became a sheep farmer, having the largest flock in the state and another in Oakland, California. It was reported that he purchased farm animals from none other than Prince Albert of England. Jewett was a successful businessman and Vermont legislator, but the Spiritualist movement would turn him into a man of other unworldly traits.

Jewett attended the séances frequently held at the Eddy home in Chittenden, becoming fully engrossed in the phenomena that were taking the world by storm. In the 1860s, he turned his talents toward healing with spiritual magnetism, advertising his uncanny ability in local newspapers as Dr. Solomon Jewett. His claims ranged from healing bad habits to fatal diseases, and his charge was quite a lot for the day.

He traveled west for a spell, and upon returning east, he met with Wella and Lizzie "Pet" Anderson in New York. The couple claimed they could paint portraits of dead people they saw and communicated with. Jewett became convinced of their talents when they produced a painting of his deceased wife, Fidelia, who had passed several years before, leading to a long friendship between the two parties.

Something else happened while he was in New York. For reasons unclear to him, he was jailed in 1868. He was unsure if it was for bad debt, lawsuit or a fraudulent claim on his medicinal cures. Either way, after five months incarcerated, he restored to life the dead body of a fellow inmate, John Cronham.

Two days after Cronham was admitted, he began to writhe in pain before falling into convulsions on the floor of his cell. The attendant and Jewett both came to his side, and Dr. Jewett started to relax the patient with his magnetic healing method. The doctor in attendance ordered Jewett back to his cell. Five physicians could not save Cronham, and he died in front of them and the jail keeper.

Jewett was allowed to pay final respects before the body was removed to the morgue. It was then that he saw a league of angels and spirits surround him, enveloping him with power. He then boldly spoke to the people in attendance to give him but forty-five minutes, and he would restore life in the deceased man. The warden agreed, as he was in danger of losing his position. Jewett set to work praying and then passing his hands over the corpse. He moved slowly at first, and at a distance, but as his magnetic power increased, he moved his hands closer, praying and breathing his life force into the dead man's mouth.

As he continued this process, he noticed the eyes twitch, move to the left and then straight forward. He continued forcing breath into Cronham's body until the man began to gasp and choke. It took only fifteen minutes for the lifeless body of John Cronham to be resuscitated. Dr. Jewett sat the man up and beckoned for the others. Upon entering the room, the crowd realized they had just witnessed a miracle. Cronham then spoke, saying, "I have been a great way off, I have seen many things." The warden called for Cronham's wife to take her husband home.

Less than one month later, Jewett was granted an unconditional release. He met up with Wella Anderson, but Wella had suffered a stroke and could not paint. Within ten minutes, Jewett cured his friend of the infliction. Jewett settled in Rutland, where he built a specific Spiritualist home. Guided by the spirits, he built an octagonal house two stories tall, complete with a spirit cabinet and a gallery of spirit portraits painted by his friend Wella.

Many were skeptical of Jewett's abilities and often tried to test them. The mainstream wannabes called him a fraud, but the doctor never let his clientele down.

Solomon Jewett died in Santa Barbara, California, on October 30, 1894, at the age of eighty-six. He was brought back to his hometown of Weybridge, Vermont, and there lies in repose in the Weybridge Hill Cemetery. The octagonal home he named Shepard Home still stands in Rutland and is a private residence.

# Nelly Butler: First Lady of American Ghosts

August 9, 1799, came and went in Sullivan, Maine, just like any other day—well, almost. Abner Blaisdel and his family were finishing their evening meal when they began to hear knocking from the basement. Upon investigation, Abner found the small chamber to be empty, yet the banging continued. In fact, it resumed every day at the same time through autumn, well into winter, until Abner, tired of his family being terrorized by an unseen force, ran down into the basement and yelled, "What do you want?"

A voice came out of the void claiming she was the ghost of Nelly Butler, Captain George Butler's deceased wife. The voice continued to speak, but Abner heard none of it, as he was already rushing up the stairs and out of the basement. Abner was in disbelief until the spirit spoke again, this time in front of the whole family.

Eleanor "Nelly" Hooper, born on April 25, 1776, was the second of nine children born to David and Joanna Hooper. At the age of nineteen, she met George Butler, a young sea captain from a relatively well-to-do family. The two were married, and within two years, Nelly was pregnant. Unfortunately, both Nelly and the baby succumbed to complications during delivery. Nelly died on June 13, 1797, and was buried on Butler Point in an unmarked grave.

Having little choice in the matter, Abner called upon David Hooper, Nelly's father, who lived a few miles from the Blaisdel home. Hooper wrote off the episode as a nightmare or fanciful dream but was soon convinced to trek out to the Blaisdel residence to check out the situation. The two repaired to the cellar, and without delay, Nelly spoke. Mr. Hooper later wrote, "She gave such clear and irresistible tokens of her being the spirit of my own daughter as gave me no less satisfaction than admiration and delight."

Nelly's ghost appeared for the first time to Abner's son Paul. As the young man walked through the fields, she floated down from the sky and hovered in front of him. He became terrified and fled for his life, but the apparition of Nelly followed close behind. She would later reprimand him for not greeting her more cordially but went on to say she would no longer scare the children.

As word spread of the strange haunting, people began to come from near and far to see or hear the ghost. The Blaisdels welcomed all who wanted to witness the phenomenon, even allowing them to camp in the front yard. Before the year had passed, more than one hundred curious folks had witnessed Nelly's ghost, either in person or voice. Many gave sworn testimony regarding their experiences. One particular witness, Mrs. Mary Gordon, wrote in her testimony that Nelly first came to the small group in the cellar as a voice "shrill but mild and pleasant." She continued in her written testimony:

> *At first, the apparition was a mere mass of light; then grew into personal form, about as tall as myself. We stood in two ranks about four or five feet apart. Between these ranks she slowly passed and re-passed, so that any of us could have handled her. When she passed by me, her nearness was that of contact; so that if there had been a substance, I should have certainly felt it. The glow of the apparition had a constant tremulous motion. At last the personal form became shapeless—expanded every way, and then vanished in a moment.*
>
> *Then I examined my own white gown and handkerchief, but I could no more see them than if they had been black.*

Reverend Abraham Cummings, the local pastor, did not believe in ghosts and felt his flock was being tricked somehow into thinking there was such a thing. He boldly rode out to the Blaisdel house with the intent to dispel any such notion of spirits and specters. While he was riding through Abner's field, a form appeared to him, "surrounded by a bright light, at first her form was no bigger than a toad." The form grew to an average human height in front of him. He immediately recognized the figure as that of Nelly Butler. The reverend was aware that Nelly had passed away during childbirth along with her child.

Nelly soon gave the reason why she was appearing to the Blaisdel family. Her widower husband was courting Lydia, Abner's daughter, and Abner was hesitant in letting her daughter, who was only fifteen at the time, marry the twenty-nine-year-old captain. However, Nelly felt that the union was inevitable and tried to convince Abner of this, stating it was her "divine mission" to see them joined in matrimony.

When asked how Nelly was aware of such knowledge, she told him, "I know all that was and will come to be." Abner decided to test her wisdom by asking her about his father. She answered that he was in heaven, praising God. Three days later, a letter arrived stating that Abner's father, who lived two hundred miles away, had passed a few days earlier.

George Butler was summoned to talk to the voice in the cellar. Upon entering the chamber, he inquired, "Who are you?"

The voice answered, "I was once your wife. Do you remember what I told you when I was alive?"

George was bewildered by the question, but Nelly continued, "Do you not remember I told you I did not think I should live long with you?…If you were to leave me, I should never wish to change my condition, but that if I was to leave you, I could not blame you if you did."

She then appeared to George in the form of a person in a winding sheet with arms folded underneath, holding a very small child. George reached out to touch the apparition, but his hand passed through it. That evening, she appeared in front of her husband two more times.

Nelly occasionally materialized in front of large groups congregated outside the Blaisdel home; traveled to neighbors' houses, where there were forty-eight spectators to prove to them that she was real; and continued to speak to her husband concerning the marriage of Lydia. It soon came to pass that Abner gave his blessing, and the union took place on May 29. After that, Nelly began to appear less frequently.

Nelly made one very ominous appearance ten days after George and Lydia were married. One night, the couple was walking home when she appeared to them, telling the newlyweds they would soon be expecting a child. Her demeanor became solemn as she warned them it would also mean the death of Lydia. She then took a sixty-three-day sabbatical before appearing almost every day in August 1800. Over one hundred people witnessed her during this point. On each occasion, she appeared in the Blaisdel cellar, preceded by knocking. Reverend Cummings later wrote that the reason she knocked before each appearance was more than likely to avoid startling anyone. He surmised that her appearing in the cellar was to allow the family to retreat to the safety of their upper chambers without the fear of being molested by the ghost.

In March 1801, Lydia and her child died during childbirth, precisely as the ghost had warned. Both were buried on Butler Point next to Nelly and her child. George Butler married a third time to a woman named Mary Googins, and they had four children from the union.

Nelly appeared only one more time, and that was in front of Reverend Cummings in his field in 1806. Reverend Cummings would later document the affair, convinced that Nelly Butler's spirit descended from heaven as a messenger of what was to come. He wrote about the event in a book called *Immortality Proved by the Testimony of Sense*.

Nelly Butler is considered to be the first documented haunting in North America. Many sworn testimonies prove that the woman came back for a reason. Either way, she became America's first lady of haunts.

## MADAME SHERRI'S STAIRCASE

Chesterfield, New Hampshire, does not seem like a place for a strange legend or story, but the small town boasts one of the most interesting sites in the region. If you should be wandering about the area, it might not be a bad idea to take a small hike into the Madame Sherri Forest. Protruding from the earth is a staircase leading toward the sky. No, it is not an apparition, but the misty figure that is seen descending the eerie flight of steps most certainly is. The staircase is part of a castle's remains once owned by Madame Antoinette Sherri, a successful costume designer from New York.

Madame Antoinette Sherri was born Antoinette Bramare in France in 1878. She changed her name in 1911 after marrying silent movie actor Andre Riela. The couple enjoyed success in their endeavors, and parties

Madame Sherri's staircase.

were frequent and full of fervor. Unfortunately, Andre died of either alcohol poison or syphilis in 1927, and Sherri decided to relocate from New York a few years after.

She purchased a sizable parcel of land containing six hundred acres in the small village of Chesterfield, New Hampshire, in the late 1920s. In 1929, she built an extravagant summer home on the property. It is reported that for years she threw wildly lavish parties there, hosting an eclectic band of friends from the big city. This vivacious woman was not shy about her partying lifestyle, nor was she reserved when it came to a public display. According to local history, she once trotted down Main Street on horseback stark naked in full Lady Godiva style, much to the townsfolk's shock and the ire of the local authorities.

Sherri purchased from the State Department a 1927 cream-colored Packard, which she drove around town attired in a large fur coat and nothing else, accompanied by none other than her pet monkey. Like many rich and famous, her extravagant glory days took a toll on her and her wealth. Her royalty checks for her work began to dwindle, and by the end of World War II, she was receiving no more.

Undaunted, Madame Sherri tried several schemes to keep her lifestyle, including turning the castle into a lavish and wild nightclub. Still, her ventures failed, and she was forced to abandon the once beautiful stone structure, which soon fell into disrepair. Sherri returned in 1959, but the locals had completely vandalized the house, with all her precious possessions and accoutrements smashed or stolen. Horrified and sad, she left the deteriorated domicile, never to return.

Sad, old and broke, she moved into the Maple Rest Nursing Home but was soon left unable to pay for her tenancy. Around 1961, she was admitted to the poor farm just outside town to spend the remainder of her days. The grand castle where she once hobnobbed with the rich and famous burned down on October 18, 1962. All that remains today is the stonework from the staircase, the foundation, columns and a fireplace. Ann Stokes later purchased the property, intending to keep the ruins intact.

Sherri died on October 21, 1965, the same day the sale of her property went through. It is these ominous-looking ruins that attract ghost hunters, historians and the curious seekers of legend. In fact, legend has it that Madame Sherri herself has been spotted atop the grand staircase, and if you listen closely, you'll hear laughter and music from her heyday echoing in the breeze around the ruins.

People often hold small personal events at the staircase, including wedding ceremonies, so if you see a party of people at the staircase, it may be those from this side of the veil. Or maybe not. The staircase is open until dark and

The foundation of Madame Sherri's home.

then gated for safety reasons, so please obey the rules. The exact nature of the danger that might lurk after dark is not specified, so you can draw your own conclusions.

## WAREHAM'S HAUNTED VIOLIN

This little clip from an article that appeared in the *Norwalk Hour* on May 4, 1967, tells it all:

*New England News Briefs*

*HAUNTED VIOLIN*

*Harold Gordon Cudworth, 61, of Wareham, Mass., is a collector of musical instruments. He thinks one of them—a 1769 Hornsteiner violin—is haunted.*

*Very often when he plays the piece called "The Broken Melody" on this violin, strange and mysterious things will happen.*

The mere fact that it made world news made this next story a legendary tale for the telling, especially since the ghost is not a misty figure roaming the dark chambers of an old mansion but rather a beautiful, ornate violin.

The Joseph Hornsteiner violin was built about 1769, presumably for a king. The 365 separate inlaid pieces mostly encompass the back of the instrument. Along the way, the instrument came into the possession of Harold Gordon Cudworth, an avid player and collector of instruments. This instrument was a bit more prized than the others not only for its beauty and sound but also its attitude toward certain musical compositions. It all started in 1945 when Cudworth first decided to play a certain tune on the instrument.

Cudworth said, "I was playing the instrument, which has a deep resonant tone at my mother's home in Wareham when suddenly a rumbling noise occurred, seemingly coming from the area of the kitchen sink."

At the time, Cudworth was playing the famous tune "The Broken Melody" by Auguste van Biene.

When Cudworth raised his bow from the strings of the violin, the noise immediately ceased. He started playing the tune where he left off, and the rumbling resumed, this time louder and more intense. The incident was strange to him, but this would only be the beginning of his experiences with the haunted violin. The following night, he repeated the song on his Hornsteiner. Not only did the rumble return, but it was accompanied by flying coffee cups and plates.

Two weeks later, he chose the Hornsteiner to practice for an upcoming concert. When he struck up "The Broken Melody," the rumbling once again resumed, but this time from above. He paused, and the noise followed suit. Cudworth stood silent, wondering what to do next. He knew it was not his imagination, as his mother had also heard the same disturbance.

Several months later, he decided to play the same tune on the Hornsteiner, but this time there was no rumble. Instead, the latch on the door to the room he was in shook violently. Cudworth left the room and started down the stairs. At that moment, the door to the room slammed shut on its own. When he returned to his room, the sheet music to "The Broken Melody" had mysteriously traveled from his music folder inside the piano bench to the music stand. This would happen on another occasion when he chose to play the same composition on the seemingly possessed violin.

Cudworth was asked to give violin lessons to a young girl in New Bedford. At the end of the lesson, the father asked Cudworth if he would perform a little melody for the family. Cudworth decided to tempt the spirits and play "The Broken Melody" on the infamous violin. As the bow ran across the strings, the rumbling began and the front door opened and closed several times, each time getting louder than the last.

A woman in Rochester, Massachusetts, called on Cudworth in 1960 to tune her piano. When she found he had a violin in the trunk of his car, she requested he play a song. He never got a chance to finish the composition before she told him never to play the song again in her presence, as it made her feel very uncomfortable. In 1966, a Mattapoisett family asked Cudworth to play a song for them on his Hornsteiner. Out of curiosity, he chose "The Broken Melody." They had to cut him off mid-song, as the pictures on the wall had begun to sway to one side, stop and sway to the other side as if they were dancing to the rhythm of the tune. He soon retired the violin into his collection but never found out the ghostly connection between the violin and "The Broken Melody."

"I am not superstitious at all," Cudworth said. "I do not believe in ghosts. But I do wish someone would explain the odd happenings this combination of violin and tune cause."

Cudworth died in 1989, and the violin might have been auctioned off with the rest of his collection. Its whereabouts remain unknown at present—unless someone decides to play a certain tune on a certain violin.

# GARDNER LAKE'S GHOSTLY PIANO

New England is full of strange stories and people. There is always an exciting legend or tale of someone or something of the more eccentric type around every turn. This next account is no exception. It is a true story that resonates to this day, not only in telling the tale but in the supernatural reverberations of music.

In southeastern Connecticut, Gardner Lake, situated on the border between Bozrah, Montville and Salem, is home to Gardner Lake State Park, located on the lake's south shore in the town of Salem. The lake is a beautiful scenic water body with an average depth of fourteen feet but is perhaps as deep as forty-plus feet in certain areas.

In February 1895, a local grocer named Thomas LeCount bought a parcel of land on the opposite side of the lake directly across from where he presently resided. He decided that he would move his family to that piece of property, as it was much nicer than where he lived at the time. He also decided to move the house, but rather than dismantling and rebuilding it, he waited until the ice was thick enough to support the house. He planned to slide the home across the lake to the new portion of land he had just acquired.

The house was lifted and dropped on sleds with oxen yokes attached. The oxen began to pull the sleds with the family home toward the south side of the lake. The venture went smoothly for a while, but the day waned quickly, and before they could get to the other side, the house slid into a large snowdrift on the ice. LeCount decided to leave the house for the night and tackle the problem in the light of day. However, mill operators, unaware that the house was resting on the ice, drained some of the pond's water to power their enterprises, causing the ice to crack and leaving the house partially submerged at a steep angle.

Because of the condition of his house, LeCount could not move it as planned. He took everything he could reach from inside the house for safekeeping. There it sat until spring, when the thaw caused it to sink in about fifteen feet of water. For years, the second story and attic remained above water. People fished from it, investigated it and even skated through it in the winter. Over time, the house sank, becoming completely submerged underwater.

Many of the large items, such as furniture, stoves and an upright piano, could not be removed and sank with the home. Now, years after the building has settled into its watery grave, divers have attested that the house and its

A postcard of the LeCount home on Gardner Lake. *Photo by Arlene Nicholson from the authors' collection.*

contents are still in a remarkable state of preservation, especially the upright piano still leaning in its original place against the parlor wall.

The instrument seems to be possessed by something no one can explain. Fishermen and others who have ventured out near the sunken house have heard the eerie echoes of soft piano music filling their ears. The muffled music breaks the tranquil silence yet does not come from the shore, but from below. Deep below. No one has ever been able to explain how or why the piano plays. Many fishermen or recreational boaters have returned from the house's area scratching their heads in astonishment, relating the sudden occurrence of soft piano music that sounded like it was emanating from below them where the house rests all but quietly at the bottom of the lake.

Take a visit to Gardner Lake and listen for yourself. If you are an experienced scuba diver, you may want to venture down into the house and perhaps catch a glimpse of the instrument or discover who may be tickling the ivories of the sunken ghostly piano.

# Bibliography

Abbott, Katherine. *Old Paths and Legends of New England.* New York: G.P. Putnam and Sons, 1907.

Babson, Roger W., and Foster H. Saville. *Cape Ann Tourists Guide.* MA: Business Statistic Organization Inc., 1936.

Bell, Michael E. *Food for the Dead.* New York: Carroll & Graf Publishers, 2001.

Boisvert, Donald J. "Rhode Island Vampires, Eerie Spirits and Ghostly Apparitions." *Rhode Island Magazine* 2, no. 9 (October 1992).

Bolte, Mary, and Mary Eastman. *Haunted New England.* Riverside, CT: Chatham Press Inc., 1972.

Botkin, B.A. *A Treasury of New England Folklore.* New York: Crown Publisher, 1944.

Carson, Gerald. *Country Stores in Early New England.* Meriden, CT: Meriden Gravure Company, 1955.

*The Celebration of the One Hundred and Fiftieth Anniversary of the Primitive Organization of the Congregational Church and Society: in Franklin, Connecticut, October 14th, 1868.* New Haven, CT: Tuttle, Morehouse, and Taylor, 1868.

Churchill, Gordon W. *Cemeteries of Cavendish, Vermont.* N.p.: Mary Churchill Publisher, 1976.

Citro, Joseph. *Cursed in New England.* Guilford, CT: Globe Pequot Press, 2004.

———. *Green Mountain Dark Tales.* Hanover, NH: University Press of New England, 1999.

*Confession of Michael Martin or Captain Lightfoot Who Was Hung at Cambridge, Massachusetts in the Year 1821, for the Robbery of Maj. Bray. Also, an Account of Dr. John Wilson, Who Recently Died at Brattleboro, VT, Believed by Many to Be the Notorious Captain Thunderbolt.* Brattleboro, VT: J.B. Miner Publisher, 1847.

Cummings, Abraham. *Immortality Proved by the Testimony of Sense.* Portland, ME: J.L. Lovell, 1859.

Cutter, Calvin. *Murder of Caroline H. Cutter by the Baptist Ministers and Baptist Churches.* Nashua, NH, 1843.

Daggett, John, and Amelia Daggett Sheffield. *A Sketch of the History of Attleborough from Its Settlement to Its Division.* Boston: Samuel Usher, 1894.

D'Agostino, Thomas. *Haunted Rhode Island.* Atglen, PA: Schiffer Publishing, 2005.

D'Agostino, Thomas, and Arlene Nicholson. *A Guide to Haunted New England.* Charleston, SC: The History Press, 2009.

Drake, Samuel A. *A Book of New England Legends and Folk Lore in Prose and Poetry.* Boston: Little, Brown and Company, 1883.

Gray, T.M. *Ghosts of Maine.* Atglen, PA: Schiffer Publishing, 2008.

Greene, J.R. *Strange Tales from Old Quabbin.* Athol, MA: Highland Press, 1993.

Griffen, Ellen M. *Moll Pitcher's Prophesies or an American Sibyl.* Boston: Eastman Press, 1895.

Griswold, S.S. *Historical Sketch of the Town of Hopkinton.* Hope Valley, RI: L.W.A. Cole, 1877.

LaMothe, Zachary. *Connecticut Lore: Strange, Off-Kilter and Full of Surprises.* Atglen, PA: Schiffer Publishing, 2013.

LaPlante, John Guy. ValleyNewsNow.Com. August 13, 2011.

Mann, Charles E. *In the Heart of Cape Ann or the Story of Dogtown.* Gloucester, MA: Procter Brothers Publishing, 1891.

Martin, Michael. *The Confession of Michael Martin or, Captain Lightfoot Who Was Hung at Cambridge, Massachusetts, in the Year 1821, for the Robbery of Maj. Bray.* VT: J.B. Miner, 1847.

Matthews, Margery I. *So I've Been Told: Stories of Foster.* Foster, RI: Foster Preservation Society, 1985.

Ocker, J.W. *The New England Grimpendium.* VT: Countryman Press, 2010.

O'Connor, Marianne. *Haunted Hikes of New Hampshire.* Exeter, NH: Publishing Works Inc., 2008.

Olcott, Henry S. *People from the Other World.* VT: Charles E. Tuttle Company, 1875.

Peterson, Pam Matthias. *Marblehead Myths, Legends and Lore.* Charleston, SC: The History Press, 2007.

*Reader's Digest*. "Strange Stories, Amazing Facts of America's Past." 1989.

Revai, Cheri. *Haunted Massachusetts*. Mechanicsburg, PA: Stackpole Books, 2005.

Rogak, Lisa. *Stones and Bones of New England*. Guilford, CT: Globe Pequot Press, 2004.

Skinner, Charles M. *Myths and Legends of Our Own Land*. Philadelphia: J.P. Lippincott Company, 1896.

Tanner, M.O. *The Witches of Jerimoth Hill* Greenville, RI: Observer Publications, 1972.

Thomas, Tracey. *Hartford Courant,* June 1, 1996.

Thomson, William O. *Coastal Ghosts and Lighthouse Lore*. Kennebunk, ME: 'Scapes Me, 2001.

Yankee Publishing. *Mad and Magnificent Yankees*. Dublin, NH: Yankee Inc., 1973.

## *Other Sources*

AtlasObscura.com

brattleborohistory.com/cemeteries/dr-john-wilson

damnedct.com

digitalvermont.org

discovermonadnock.com

Find-A-Grave.com

www.murderbygaslight.com

"Old Coot." North Adams transcript, March 9, 1971.

*Princeton Alumni Weekly* 44 (September 10, 1943).

www.seacoastnh.com

www.wikipedia.org

# About the Authors

Thomas D'Agostino and his wife, Arlene Nicholson, have been extensively studying and investigating paranormal accounts for over thirty-nine years, with over 1,400 investigations to their credit. Tom and Arlene are ardent researchers of New England history, haunts, legends and folklore. Creators of fourteen books, together they have penned and captured on film the best haunts and history New England has to offer.

Tom and Arlene's interviews and paranormal experiences have appeared in numerous newspapers, magazines and other periodicals throughout New England and beyond in regard to their books and comprehensive work in the paranormal field.

Tom has contributed to other various books and publications and has appeared on many television and radio shows, as well as documentaries on the subject of the paranormal. Tom is a graduate of Rhode Island College with a degree in political science. He is a professional teacher and musician. Tom builds his own musical instruments, many from the Medieval and Renaissance periods, that are used in his profession.

Arlene is a professional photographer with a degree in photography.

*Visit us at*
www.historypress.com